Eldritchwood

A Solo Adventure Game by Andrea Sfiligoi and Anna Pashchenko

Layout and graphics: Andrea Sfiligoi

Playtesting and useful comments: Andrea Sfiligoi, Anna Pashchenko, Sergio Laliscia, Daniel Casquilho, Simone Peruzzi, and all the players who tested it at Lucca Games and Modena Play.

Proofreading: Marty Costello

www.ganeshagames.net

Table of Contents

Introduction	1
The Story	1
Dice	2
Game Terms and Rules	3
Characters	5
Dice Tests	5
Advantage and Disadvantage	5
Rerolls	6
Fate Points	6
Persuading People	6
Combat Encounters	6
Death Scenes	7
Social Combat	7
Conditions	7
Death Table	7
Escalation Table	8
Disease	9
Scandal	9
Wanted	9
Spells	9
White Magic	9
Athame	9
Clean the Mind	9
Cleanse Wounds	9
Create Alraune	10
Determination	10
Discover Secret	10
Find Hidden Things	10
Find the Path	10
Healing	10
Iron Amulet against the Fae	10
Protection from Wounds	10
Repel Pest	10
Purification	10
Ritual Circle	10
Sobriety	10

Talisman Against Shadows	10
Red Magic	11
Fascination	11
Greek Fire	11
Instill Passion	11
Lightning Strike	11
Love Philter	11
Sterility	11
Black Magic	11
Evil Eye	11
Familiar	11
Hand of Glory	11
Homunculus	11
Invisibility Beans	12
Summon Goblin	12
Spiritual Assault	12
Speak with the Dead	12
Spread Disease	12
Summon Demon	12
Scourge of the Dead	14
Witch's flight	14
Witch's Ladder	14
Actions	14
Accuse	15
Assassination	15
Attend Social Event	15
Attend Sunday Mass	15
Befriend Someone	16
Blackmail	16
Black Market	16
Buy	16
Challenge to Duel	17
Court	17
Gather Firewood	17
General Market	17
Gossip	18

Table of Contents

Hunt	19
Investigate	19
Pick Mushrooms	19
Raid the Graveyard	19
Resting	20
Pray	20
Read	20
Rescue from Prison	20
Search for herbs	20
Sell Stolen Goods	20
Stroll through the Forest	21
Theft	21
Use Trait	21
Visit the Apothecary	21
Visit a Friend	21
Visit the Goldsmith	21
Visit the Herbalist	21
Visit the Moneylender	21
Visit the Tavern	22
The Notables	23
Creating Your Own Character	60
Major Foes	61
Dangers	67
How to Play	92
Important Calendar Dates	92
Events Track	94
Scenes	101

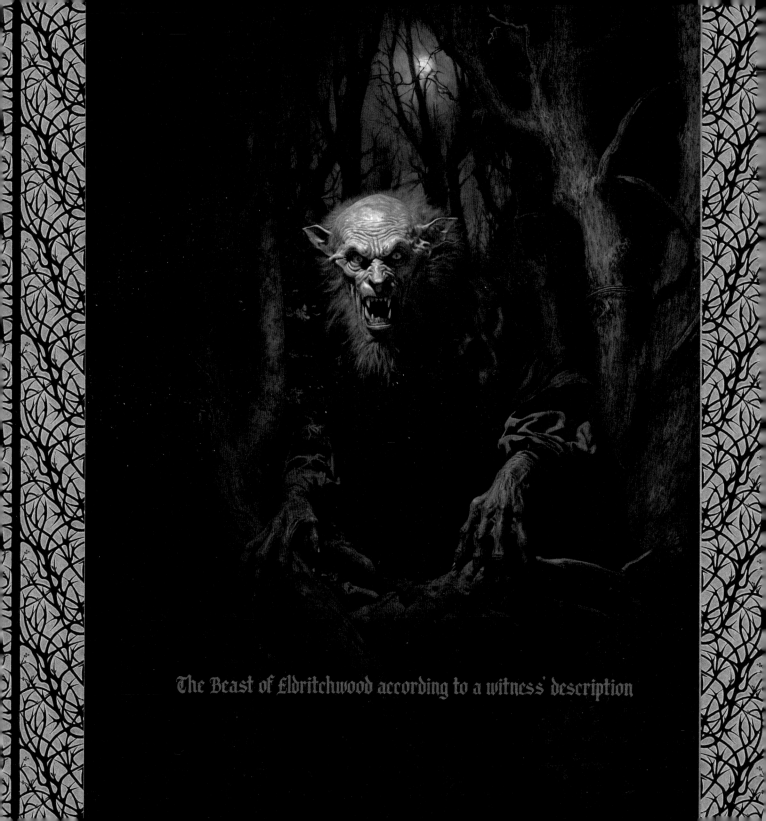

The Beast of Eldritchwood according to a witness' description

Rules of the Game

Introduction

This is a solo adventure game. You play as the Notables of Eldritchwood - a group of 36 unusual characters in a (not-historically accurate) medieval European village besieged by the forces of evil. You don't play all the characters at once - just like in a TV series the camera would move from one character to another as the story develops, you control one character at a time. The character you are controlling is called the Acting character. A character will often involve other characters in a scene, and when this happens, you may switch to the other character. The characters' actions and your choices will guide the story and determine whether Eldritchwood survives or falls prey to the forces of evil. You win the game if the supernatural menace threatening Eldritchwood is defeated.

The Story

Eldritchwood is a small village on the edge of a large forest, which is home to plenty of game but also of supernatural presences that gave the village its name. The supernatural creatures make wandering through the woods dangerous. The forest was once the realm of a couple of fey creatures, the two-headed King of Thorns and his beloved spouse, the Whispering Queen. The two have now separated and despise each other with a passion. They both want to be left alone and resent the presence of humans in their realm.

The forest is also the place of choice for dark rituals performed by pagans whose aim is to destroy Christianity and reinstate the Old Ways.

A river runs through Eldritchwood and opens into a swampy area near the South town gate. Agatha, a

Agatha's Swamp

witch, has made the swamp her home. The Inquisition has tried multiple times to destroy her, but the forces of Nature seem to be at her command. In addition, she has amassed a small army of undead – the reanimated corpses of the men who were claimed by the baleful exhalations of the swamp and the dangerous wildlife of the forest. To make things even worse, the swamp has become the home of a dragon-like creature, a large reptile that seems to thrive in the noxious miasmas.

On a hill far from the village rises the castle of Countess Elizabeth, who survived her husband (who was taken by the Plague) thanks to unholy magic that has made her dependent on frequent baths in the blood of virgins. Many say the Countess is a revenant. Only a shadow of her former beauty remains in her soulless stare. Her evil ways have attracted other monstrosities – the most recent a savage werewolf, whose night-time howls curdle the villagers' blood.

Dice

To play this game, you need a couple of standard six-sided dice, called d6 . If the rules tell you to roll d6+1, it means "roll a die and add 1 to the result". One special type of die roll is the d66 roll. To roll d66, you roll the d6 twice, counting the first number rolled as the "tens" and the second number rolled as the

"units", thus generating a number from 11 to 66. This is useful when the rules tell you to select a random character or danger (all characters and dangers have a corresponding number, 11 to 66, on their profile).

Countess Elizabeth's Castle

Rules of the Game

Game Terms and Rules

Game jargon may sound unusual to first-time players. If you read this alphabetical list carefully, you will learn the most important rules.

D3: Roll a six-sided die and count 1-2 as 1, 3-4 as 2 and 5-6 as 3, thus generating a number from 1 to 3.

D6: Roll a six-sided die.

D66: Roll a six-sided die twice, counting the first number as "tens" and the second as "units", thus generating a number 11 to 66. You may also roll two differently-colored d6s at the same time, always reading one color as "tens" and the other as "units".

Action: An Action is something IMPORTANT that your character does over the course of a day. This does not mean that performing the action takes the whole day. The action is the most noteworthy thing about the character that day. In game terms a character performs 1 Action per day. Actions include things such as buying a specific item, courting an attractive person, looking for information, reading a book, studying magic, going to the forest to pick up healing herbs, attending Church, and so on. Some Actions take more than one day to complete. *For example, reading a book may take several days.*

Combat encounter: A moment in the game where two characters attack each other with the intent to maim, kill or capture each other. In combat, fighting against a group of foes is just like fighting against a single character. For example, if you fight a group of guards, you treat them as a single entity.

Cooperative Play: If there is more than one player, one additional Major Foe per additional player will be attacking the village. Up to 6 players can play at the same time. The overall rules are unchanged. The only limitation is that a player may not control a character controlled by another player unless both players agree to Switch control of their characters.

Dangers: Dangers include animals, bandits, thieves, and natural obstacles such as inclement weather. Dangers are numbered 11 to 66, letting you select a random one with a d66 roll when the need arises. A few Dangers have numbers higher than 66 and you cannot play them as a result of a die roll. You play them when instructed to do so by an Event or by another rule in the game.

Death: Characters in the game can succumb to disease, infection, old age, and can be killed by fellow humans, animals, or supernatural creatures. When your current character dies, you may switch to another – a Contact of the character who just died or, if no Contacts are available, another random Notable. THE STORY NEVER ENDS BECAUSE A CHARACTER DIED. The story ends only when an event tells you so.

Events: There are two lists of events – **Timed** (events that happen on specific dates in the Calendar) and events on the **Event Track**. When you roll on the event track, you roll d3 and add it to the current number on the track, and play the corresponding event.

For example, if the current Event Track is on 13 and you roll a 3, you play Event (13+3)= 16.

As time progresses, events become more dangerous. Some events will happen multiple times.

Major Foes: There are six unique Major Foes in the game: The Swamp Witch, the King of Thorns, The Whispering Queen, Countess Elisabeth, the Beast of Eldritchwood, and Salmac, the Marquis of Hell. Attacking a Major Foe unprepared means certain death for your character – you must perform certain activities and find Special Items to have a fighting chance. During your investigation, you will be given the opportunity to spend Clues to determine which of the six Major Foes is NOT the one attacking Eldritchwood. As play progresses, you eliminate one suspect after the other until you discover the identity of your true enemy.

Notables: These are the 36 most remarkable characters in the village. You begin the game playing

Rules of the Game

a random Notable and then switch to others as they are involved in the story. *For example, you could start the game playing a blacksmith and then switch to his secret lover the countess, after they have been involved in an action together.*

Random character: Roll d66 on the Notables list to select a character at random. If you select a character that is dead or unavailable for any other reason, roll again.

Reroll: Rerolling means rolling a die again when you do not like the result. Characters have a limited number of rerolls. These are part of their resources and represent characters with a better than average chance of succeeding at something because of their training or equipment. Some rerolls are limited to specific circumstances. For example, a soldier may have a few rerolls that represent his military training and that he can use only in combat situations. If a reroll is listed as Universal, it means it can be used on any die roll.

Sacrifice: To Sacrifice an Item means that the Item is lost, and the listed effect is caused. *For example, if the rules tell you to sacrifice Greek Fire to destroy a Bewitched Scarecrow, you automatically destroy the Scarecrow by using the Greek Fire. The Greek Fire is now gone.You may find that item again during the game, unless the rules tell you otherwise.*

Scene: A Scene is a moment in the game where a game resource is spent or dice are rolled to determine an outcome, or when a character uses time to perform a task.

Solo Play: The standard way to play this game is Solo. This means a single player will go through the book, using as many characters as needed until the story reaches its conclusion.

Special Item: An interesting object picked up or carried by a character. Characters are assumed to have all everyday items pertaining to their profession, daily life, attire, food, and so on. The game does not obsess over minutiae. We describe in game terms only the objects that have a special significance. These will be indicated with Capital Letters. *For example, if you find a Jar of Honey, it is a Special Item that may be useful to distract an angry bear.* **No character may carry more than 10 Special Items.** If you find more items than you can carry, you must discard some of them or give them to another character sharing a scene with you.

Spell: A game effect caused by magic. A few characters begin the game knowing a spell or two, but in most cases spells may only be learned during the game, reading instructions from Grimoires.

Switching: You do not use a single character, but you switch to another character when the story allows, just like a director would switch from one character's point of view to another in a movie as the need arises. You, however, must abide to two rules while doing so. 1) You may switch to a different character after you have involved that character in a scene. There are certain moments, for example all major holy days and Sundays, where potentially ALL characters meet and you involve another character in the story. 2) In addition, all characters have a list of Contacts – these can be involved in the story at any time using the "Visit a friend" Action.

Time: The game is played over a variable number of game days. You keep track of the passage of time by using a planner (we recycle old planners).Some timed events, like Christmas or All Hallow's Eve, happen on their specific dates (e.g., Christmas happens on December 25th). The various dates may have significance in the game, as for example supernatural creatures are stronger around Halloween. On average, your story will last 2-4 months of game time, but this largely depends on your choices and actions.

You: When the game says "you", it is just a short way of saying "the character currently played by you, the player".

4

Rules of the Game

Characters

Characters in this game are of two types: the **Notables**, also called PCs or Player-Characters because they are controlled by you, the player, and NPCs (Non-Player Characters) listed in the Major Foes or Dangers sections, so called because they are controlled by the game.

All characters in the game (both Pcs and NPCs) are defined by Attributes, numerical values that detail how strong, smart, or agile the character is. They are as follows:

Vigor: A measure of the character's physical strength and endurance, Vigor is used for feats of strength like lifting a boulder or bashing down a door, and as a measure of the character's vitality. Vigor is important for combat scenes.

Dexterity: A measure of how agile the character is, Dexterity is used to climb, dodge, move quickly, and so on. Dexterity is important for combat scenes, chases, and so on.

Mind: A measure of how smart the character is. Mind is used to understand complex things, learn quickly and solve puzzles.

Charisma: A measure of how attractive the character is, in terms of physical appearance and personality. Characters with a high Charisma will find it easier to influence the actions of others, persuading them to follow their suggestions.

Will: A measure of how strong-willed the character is. A character with a high Will score will resist mental powers, fear, torture, and sin.

Alertness: A measure of the senses of the character, Alertness will let you perceive hidden dangers, traps, or a person following you through a crowd.

Gold: A measure of the character's disposable income. All characters have means of feeding and housing themselves. You do not keep track of small daily expenses. Anyway, each character begins the game with a different amount of Gold that can be spent to obtain special goods and services. When characters run out of Gold, they have no more disposable income, but it is assumed that they can still feed themselves, pay taxes, etc.

Status: Status is a measure of the character's position in society. Peasants are Status 0, freemen are 1, well-off tradesmen and small nobles are 2, and higher ranking nobles are 3 or 4.

Milestones: Each character has different goals. These are called Milestones. When a goal is achieved, the character unlocks some positive effect as described on their profile. Each Milestone can be completed only once unless the text says otherwise.

Contacts: Each character has friendship, love, enmity or some other form of relationship with a few other characters in the game. Contacts are used to involve another character in a scene and switch from controlling a character to another during the game.

Dice Tests

Every time a character tries to perform an action that is not automatically successful, you must perform a Test. **In a Test, you always roll 1 die and try to roll a 4 or better.** This roll is modified by the difference between the Attribute you are using and the Attribute of another character who is trying to resist the action. When there is no opposing character, the rules will list a difficulty number that is used in the same way.

Example: Percival Quickfingers is trying to steal a key from a guardsman. Percival must test his Dexterity of 3 vs. the guard's Alertness of 2. Percival's Dexterity is 1 point better than his target's Alertness, so instead of needing to roll a 4 or better, Percival needs to roll a 3 or better.

No matter how good or bad you are, there is always a chance to fail or succeed. **Any roll of 1 means that the roll fails, and any roll of 6 means the roll succeeds.**

The roll is always described from the point of view of the Acting Character.

You roll for Percival's chance of stealing without being caught, NOT for the guard's chance of catching Percival red-handed.

Advantage and Disadvantage

In some cases, the rules tell you to roll with **Advantage** or **Disadvantage**. With Advantage, roll 2 dice and choose the best result. With Disadvantage, roll 2 dice and choose the worst result.

Rules of the Game

Rerolls

In some cases, characters have a resource called "rerolls" that can be used to reroll failed dice. Some rerolls are **Universal** and can be used in any circumstances. Others can be used only in specific circumstances (for example, Hunting rerolls may be used only when hunting a beast) or for a specific Attribute (for example, Will rerolls may be used only to reroll Will rolls). Unless the rules tell you otherwise, **you may reroll as many times you want, as long as you have Rerolls to use**. When you run out of rerolls, you are out of luck. Use them wisely.

You do NOT have to declare that you are going to use a reroll before rolling: you can decide to use a reroll after rolling the die and seeing that it failed.

Rerolls are a one-time resource. They do not "reset" or regenerate at any moment. Accomplishing certain actions and completing Milestones may give you Rerolls as a reward.

Fate Points

Fate Points allow you to control a character's fate, up to a point. You may spend 1 Fate point to automatically roll a 6 on any die roll in the game, including a roll on a Table. Fate points are limited: **you, the player, have a total of 10 Fate points to use in a game.** Once 1 Fate point is used, it's gone. There are a few situations, such as completing a character's Milestone, that let you gain 1 Fate.

IMPORTANT: Y**ou may not spend more than 2 total Fate points on an action that requires rolling multiple d6, for example in combat encounters, or when you are asked to test an Attribute multiple times in a row.**

Persuading People

When you want to convince someone to do something, test your Charisma vs. the target's Will. If the person has any sort of enmity with your character, as per their profile, roll with Disadvantage. If the person Loves you, roll with Advantage.

Note that being married does not necessarily equate with Love. A character could be Married to someone but love someone else.

Combat Encounters

When you are involved in a Combat, roll the best of your current Vigor or Dexterity scores vs. the best of your foe's Vigor or Dexterity. Roll 3 dice. You may use up to 2 Fate points and any rerolls as per your character's profile. Rerolls represent the effect of weapons, armor, or fighting experience. Count how many dice roll a success.

- **If you roll 3 successes,** you clearly win and destroy, kill, defeat or capture the foe, as appropriate to the scene (you choose). Your character suffers no damage.

- **If you roll 2 successes,** you Wound the foe. Reduce the foe's Vigor by 1. Your character is maybe a little scuffed up, but in game terms the character suffers no damage.

- **If you roll 1 success,** both the foe and you are Wounded. Lose 1 point of Vigor or Dexterity (your choice) and reduce the foe's Vigor or Dexterity (your choice) by 1. Some foes will not fight to the bitter end and will be defeated or run away if they are Wounded. This is written in their description.

- **If you roll no successes,** you are Seriously Wounded. Lose 2 points from any combination of Vigor and/or Dexterity.

If at the end of the process the foe is not defeated and you want to continue, repeat the process by rolling 3d6 again. You may opt to flee instead. To flee, Test your Dexterity vs. the foe's Dexterity. If you succeed, you manage to escape. If you fail, you are Wounded again (lose 1 from Vigor or Dexterity, your choice).

If your Dexterity reaches 0, you may not run away from fights until you heal your Attribute. You may still move, but your agility is severely impaired by your conditions.

If your Vigor reaches 0 or below, you pass out. Roll on the Death Table below.

Rules of the Game

Death Table (d6)

1-2	You die! You may play a Death Scene (see below) and then Switch to another character. Use a Contact of your previous character or, if you prefer, advance the calendar by d6 days and select a random Notable by rolling d66. She/he will continue the story, investigating the previous character's causes of death.
3-4	You collapse, but wake up a few hours later with a maximum of Vigor 1. All your Gold and Special Items are gone. You must rest a minimum of 1d6 days after this ordeal.
5-6	Just a Flesh Wound! You wake up with full Vigor and Dexterity, but must rest a minimum of 1 day after this ordeal.

Death Scenes

The death of a Notable may be a dramatic moment in the story. You may let the character slump to the ground and die, or test your Will vs. 1. If the test fails, nothing happens – you just die. If the test is successful, perform one of the following actions before you shuffle off this mortal coil:

Pray: You spend your last few moments praying for someone. Your next character gains 1 Universal reroll.

Leave a Clue. You manage to leave a Clue (for example, scribbling the name of your killer with your blood) that will be helpful to the next character. Your next character gains 1 Clue.

Hide a Special Item. You manage to hide a single Special Item in a way that your next character will find it later. Your other possessions are stolen or otherwise lost.

Dying Blow. You manage to roll another Combat die, at +2 to your Vigor or Dexterity (choose). Apply the result as normal, but you will die anyway at the end of the process. This may be useful to deal a killing blow to a dangerous unique foe to take him/her out of the game. This is a single die, not 3 dice as in a normal Combat resolution, and the only effect is to inflict 1 Wound to the foe, if the die roll is successful. If you have any rerolls available, use them for the Dying Blow. You may also use 1 Fate to make sure the Dying Blow hits (this may lead to a conclusion where the hero dies but his/her sacrifice is enough to slay the bad guy).

Social Combat

Social combat happens in situations where characters try to put down, offend, bully or humiliate each other. It may escalate into physical combat in rare circumstances. Whenever your character initiates Social Combat, test your Charisma, Mind or Status against your opponent's Charisma, Mind or Status three times. Use the best Attribute for both characters. Apply the following results:

3 Successes: The opponent is Humiliated. S/he must leave the scene and now becomes an Enemy of the character. The character is clearly perceived as the victor in the social conflict.

2 Successes: You win the Social Combat, but you don't cast off a good impression, and lose some confidence. You will be at -1 to whatever Attribute you use for a Social Conflict in the next d6 days.

1 Success: You win the Social Combat, but you must test your Will vs. the opponent's Charisma or Mind (the higher of the two). If the roll is successful, nothing happens. If it fails, roll on the Escalation Table on next page.

No successes: You lose the Social Combat, must leave the scene and are Humiliated. See Conditions, below.

Conditions

Effects on your character (such as being drunk, in love, bewitched, etc.) are called Conditions. Each Condition is a rule that can be removed using certain resources, or will disappear after some time.

Wounded: Being Wounded implies the loss of points from Dexterity and/or Vigor. When a loss is indicated, assign this loss to Vigor or Dexterity as you prefer. If the character suffers the loss of 2 points, you can assign 1 point to Vigor and 1 on Dexterity, or deduct both points from the same Attribute. The Wounded Condition is removed by Healing. Each point of lost Vigor or Dexterity will take (1d6 minus Vigor) days of rest to heal. Reduce the number of days by 1 if you buy a treatment from an apothecary or herbalist (1 Gold per day of treatment). A Disease will last a minimum of 1 day.

Drunk: A Drunk character is at Disadvantage on all Mind, Dexterity and Will tests. This Condition disappears after 1 day.

In Love: You may be in Love as a result of a successful seduction attempt or because your character has found True Love. A character who is in Love gets 1 free reroll every week. If the relationship ends or the loved one dies, you must choose between becoming Drunk for d6 days, Weak or Morose.

Poisoned: A Poisoned character must perform a Vigor roll vs. 1 every day, before the character has a chance to perform any action for that day. As soon as the character rolls a success, the Poisoned Condition is removed. If the roll fails, the character loses 1 point of Vigor or Dexterity (your choice). You may also purchase an antidote at the apothecary (character 25) or at the herbalist (character 46) for 5 Gold. Taking the antidote gives you 1 reroll on any Vigor roll against the poison for the next 3 attempts.

Characters 25 and 46 get the antidote for free if they need it for themselves.

The Poisoned condition is cumulative: characters may have multiple doses of poison in their body, and they must perform a Vigor roll for each.

Weak: A Weak character may not use reroll on any Vigor or Dexterity roll. The Weakened condition is removed after d6 minus Vigor days of rest, with a minimum of 1 day. To rest, the character must perform the "rest" action and do nothing else than reading on those days.

Humiliated: A Humiliated character has -1 on Charisma and all Social Combat until s/he completes a Milestone. As soon as a Milestone is completed, humiliated characters restore faith in themselves and remove the condition. Note that the other effects of completing the Milestone still apply.

Morose: A Morose character may not use rerolls until you remove the Condition. It will naturally disappear after d6xd6 days, or as soon as the character completes a Milestone.

Bewitched: A Bewitched character becomes susceptible to all supernatural effects, and rolls at Disadvantage to resist any spell or magic effect. The only ways to remove the Bewitched Condition is to attend (or perform) mass on Sunday, or to use a Purification spell (see Spells, below).

Excommunicated: A character who is Excommunicated may no longer attend mass, marry, or gain any benefit from Prayer, Holy water or Holy relics.

Escalation Table (d6)	
1-3	You become Morose. See Conditions.
4-5	The conflict becomes a physical assault. Fight a round of combat (a single die). Any Wound suffered in this fight will not be fatal and will automatically heal after d6-Vigor days (minimum 1 day).
6	Duel! If you are a man or any character described as armed, you must fight a regular Combat (3 dice) against your opponent. However, if your opponent is of higher Status than you, the opponent will ignore the challenge unless you successfully test Charisma vs. the opponent's Will. If you are a priest, you will not fight but you become Morose until the opponent is Excommunicated or dies. If you are a woman, you become Morose until your opponent is killed (including by Assassination), Excommunicated, Jailed or Humiliated. It does not matter if these Conditions are caused directly by you or by another character (for example, you could have a priest excommunicate your enemy or have him killed by an assassin).

Rules of the Game

Disease

When a character risks contracting a disease, the character must test Vigor vs. that disease's number. On a failure, apply the effects of the disease. Infectious diseases can spread easily in the game, especially if the outbreak happens during festivals and other social events. Treatment can be provided by an apothecary or herbalist or by the Healing spell.

Scandal

If you are involved in something that causes Scandal, you may not participate in social events until you spend 1 Fate or complete one of the character's Milestones. In some cases, Scandal equates with the character's "social death", so it may be sensible to leave the character alone and switch to another character. In a medieval society, people acting out of societal norms were ostracized and shunned.

Scandal can be caused by a Secret being revealed, like being in an adulterous or same-sex relationship, being jailed, being accused of witchcraft or any serious crime that could be punished with death.

Wanted

If a character becomes Wanted, he or she may participate only in illegal activities and in activities that do not involve interaction with other characters. From now on, whenever the character rolls a 1 on any roll in a social situation (whenever the character is interacting with other characters), Guards will arrive and try to apprehend the character (play Danger 23).

Spells

In certain circumstances, you may acquire handwritten magical tomes called Grimoires. Grimoires can be studied to learn Spells. When you purchase a Grimoire, roll d6 to determine what type of magic it contains: **1-3 White, 4-5 Red, 6 Black**. Then roll d6 minus 1 (with a minimum of 1) to determine how many spells it contains. Then determine which spells it contains rolling on the appropriate list (White, Red or Black).

Learning spells takes time. Roll 2d6 minus the character's Mind to calculate how many days are needed to study the spell. At the end of the process,

perform a Mind roll vs. 2. On a failure, you didn't learn the spell. You may start again if you want. On a success, you learn the spell. From now on, you can use that spell as many times as you want. Each spell has different rules and requirements, described below.

All spells, benign or malign, attract the attention of the supernatural entities around Eldritchwood. **Every time a spell is cast, you must advance the Events Track by d6.**

Possessing any Grimoire is considered a Secret. If this is revealed, it will make the character a Suspect for the Inquisition, and may lead to imprisonment, torture and being burned at the stake as a witch.

Spells are divided into Red, Black and White. Some characters may gain additional spells as part of one of their Milestones when they collect a certain number of Grimoires.

Secret Words: When you buy or find a grimoire, you may decide that it contains a single Secret Word instead of spells. Knowing THREE Secret Words is needed to encounter the King of Thorns.

White Magic (roll d66 for a random Spell)

- ### 11-12-13 Athame

The caster creates an Athame, an enchanted knife. The caster may use the Athame once per game to automatically reduce by 1 the Will or Vigor of a single encountered supernatural creature. Possession of an Athame gives the caster Advantage on Will rolls when dealing with demons summoned by the caster.

- ### 14-15 Clean the Mind

Casting this spell instantly heals all lost points of Will or Mind on a single character.

- ### 16-21-22 Cleanse Wounds

Casting this spell instantly heals 1 point of lost Vigor or Dexterity from a single character.

Rules of the Game

- **23 Create Alraune**

Casting this spell, you carve a mandrake root into an *alraune*, a female figurine that will protect a house. The protected person is now immune to Spiritual Assault and Witch's Ladder. You need to find a mandrake root (Danger 79) to complete this spell.

- **24- 25 Determination**

Casting this spell gives Advantage to the caster's next Will roll.

- **26- 31-32 Discover Secret**

Casting this spell, the caster gains 1 Clue or 1 of the Secret Words needed to summon the King of Thorns (see Major Foes).

- **33-34-35 Find Hidden Things**

Casting this spell makes you find 1 Clue that you may use only to find a hidden treasure or item (this may also reveal an item hidden by a character during a Dying Action. If the caster doesn't know of any hidden treasure when the spell is cast, the caster will find 5 Gold instead.

- **36-41 Find the Path**

Casting this spell, a caster who is lost will automatically find the way home.

- **42-43-44-45 Healing**

Casting this spell frees a single person (the caster or another person, who must be present at the moment of casting) from a disease. Casting the spell requires paying 5 Gold to an apothecary or herbalist. This cost is waived if the caster is an apothecary or herbalist.

- **46-51 Iron Amulet against the Fae**

This spell creates an amulet that keeps the fae at bay. Building the amulet costs 10 Gold and the work of a skilled blacksmith (e.g., Character 21) is required. The wearer of the amulet may ignore an encounter or event with any fairy creature by performing a successful Will roll vs. the Will of the fairy creature.

- **52-53 Protection from Wounds**

Cast this spell on yourself or on another character, who must be present at the moment of casting. The character will ignore 1 Wound in the next Combat or event played.

- **54 Repel Pest**

Casting this spell lets you avoid an encounter with Rats or Ravens.

- **55-56 Purification**

Casting this spell purifies the soul of the caster. From now on, until the caster takes a human life or casts a Black magic spell, when the caster casts a spell, the caster advances the Events track by d6-1, not d6, to a minimum of 1. Multiple castings do not have a cumulative effect, but a caster who has lost the purified status may reinstate it with another casting.

- **61-62-63 Ritual Circle**

Casting the Ritual Circle is tiring, and reduces the caster's Will by 1 for 1d6 days. If the caster's Will is 1, the caster loses 1 Vigor instead. The lost Vigor and Will may not be healed by magic, but only by rest. When the character casts a spell from within the Circle, the caster advances the Events track by d6-1, not d6, to a minimum of 1. This is cumulative with the effects of the Purification spell, so a character casting a spell from a Circle after Purification reduces the Event Track roll by 2.

- **64 Sobriety**

Casting this spell cancels the Drunk condition on a single character immediately.

- **65-66 Talisman Against Shadows**

This ritual teaches the caster how to build a Talisman against shadows, spending 5 Gold in materials. Any character wearing such a Talisman is immune to the Spiritual Assault spell.

Rules of the Game

Red Magic (roll d6 for a random Spell)

- **1 Fascination**

Casting this spell gives Advantage to the caster's next Charisma roll.

- **2 Greek Fire**

You learn the secret to create a highly flammable liquid. Creating 1 dose of Greek Fire will cost you 15 Gold in raw materials and 1d6 days of work.

- **3 Instill Passion**

Using this spell, the caster performs a Will roll vs. the Will of a victim. If the caster wins, the next attempt at seducing the victim will be rolled with Advantage.

- **4 Lightning Strike**

Using this spell, you cause a target to be struck by lightning and die. The character's death will look like it was caused by a natural event. You may use this spell only once in the game, and not against any supernatural foes.

- **5 Love Philter**

Casting this spell and spending 4 Gold in materials, the user creates a potion that, when imbibed by a victim, will make that person fall in love with the next suitable person encountered. This can be one of the caster's contacts, or another character that is meeting the person who drank the potion. Slipping the potion into a drink requires a Dexterity roll vs. the victim's Alertness. On a failure, the victim will be alerted and the caster will be Suspected of witchcraft. The caster may also create the potion and sell it to another character (for a cost of 15 Gold). The buyer is then responsible for performing the Dexterity roll to have the victim imbibe the potion.

- **6 Sterility**

Casting this spell on a character makes for that character impossible to conceive children. Ignore any pregnancy event for that character (if she's a woman) or for any woman with whom he has a relationship with (if he is a man) unless the woman is having a secret affair with another man.

Black Magic (roll d66 for a random Spell)

- **11 Evil Eye**

This spell lets you bring bad luck to others. You may use it to have a person's pet die, or to bring them financial misfortune: the target loses a number of Gold equal to d6 times its Status, to a minimum of 1d6 Gold. Every time you use this spell to attack someone, perform a Mind roll vs. the target's Alertness. If you fail, the person will understand that something supernatural is occurring.

- **12 Familiar**

This spell lets you summon a spirit in the form of a pet, typically a cat or raven, that follows you everywhere. While the familiar is with you, you get the chance to reroll any failed Alertness roll. If for any reason the familiar dies, you permanently lose 1 Vigor.

- **13-14-15 Hand of Glory**

This ritual lets you build a Hand of Glory, a necromantic Special Item. To build the Hand, you need the hand of a dead person (you must either be present at the death of a character, or play the Pilfer the Graveyard action to retrieve a hand from a grave). If you carry the Hand of Glory, you will be able to reroll any attempt to pick a lock. In addition, once per game, you may use the Hand of Glory to paralyze any foe with a Charisma roll vs. the target's Will and run away or take any object in that person's possession. You may also kill the paralyzed person. If the roll fails, you must fight your target instead. If you are caught with a hand of Glory in your possession, you will be automatically put to trial by the Inquisition. The Hand of Glory does not work on animals and undead targets.

- **16-21-22 Homunculus**

Preparation for this spell is laborious and time-consuming. The caster must lose 1 point of Vigor or Dexterity and work on building the homunculus for 30 days. The lost point of Vigor or Dexterity cannot be healed until the period of creation ends. Once the homunculus is created, at any point in the game, the caster may use the homunculus to heal up to 3 points of Vigor and/or Dexterity, or to gain 6 rerolls. Using

the homunculus kills it. A caster may have a single homunculus at any given moment of the game.

- **23-24-25-26 Invisibility Beans**

The caster must pay a visit to the graveyard and steal the head of a dead person. This requires successfully playing the Raid the Graveyard action. After the caster has a head, the caster must place d6 beans in its mouth, bury it and water it for 7 days. Upon the dawn of the 8th day, the caster retrieves the beans from the mouth of the dead head. When a bean is placed into the caster's mouth, the caster gains Advantage on all rolls to avoid detection (being seen or heard) or can automatically avoid capture or flee from a combat without suffering any consequences. Each bean may be used only once, and the spell may not be cast again until all beans have been used.

- **31-32 Summon Goblin**

The caster creates a goblin thought-form and sends it against a target (this must be a character that the caster has interacted with at least once in the game) to steal one object. Treat as a Theft attempt. The goblin has a score of 1 on all Attributes. If the Theft attempt succeeds, the caster will find the stolen object under their pillow on the following morning. If the attempt fails, the goblin disappears. A new goblin will refuse to try to steal the same object. The goblin cannot steal anything from any character who has a Splendid Housecat as a pet.

- **33-34-35 Spiritual Assault**

The caster creates a shadow of pure hate and sends it against a target (this must be a character that the caster has interacted with at least once in the game). Treat as an Assassination attempt. The shadow creature has 2 on all Attributes. If the attempt succeeds, the target character will be found dead in his sleep, as if he dies of a heart attack. If the attempt fails, the shadow disappears. A new shadow will refuse to try to kill the same target. The shadow creature cannot assassinate any character possessing a Talisman against Shadows.

- **36-41-42 Speak with the Dead**

This spell may be cast on a Notable that has died over the course of the game. The caster gains 1 Clue with a successful Will roll vs. the Will of the deceased character.

- **43-44 Spread Disease**

This spell may be cast against a chosen victim, also over a distance, without the victim knowing, to make sure the victim falls ill. The caster must roll Will vs. the victim's Vigor. If the roll is successful, the victim falls ill and will have to be in bed for d6 days. At the end of this period, roll again, until the caster fails the Will vs. Vigor roll. At that point, the disease ends. The victim may also be healed before the end of the disease by the Healing spell (see White magic).

- **45-46-51-52 Summon Demon**

The caster learns how to summon a minor demon. Upon completion of the ritual, which requires the expenditure of 4 Gold in materials, the caster must perform a Combat encounter with a Minor Demon (play Danger 34). Use the caster's Mind and Will instead of the caster's Vigor and Dexterity in the combat. If the caster is Wounded, apply the loss of 1 point of Will or Mind or Charisma instead of a loss of Vigor or Dexterity. Like in regular combat, you decide which Attributes are reduced. Per every loss the caster suffers, advance the Event Track by d6. In any case, after the combat, the demon will either disappear (if the demon won) or comply with the caster's wishes (if the caster won), as described below. If the caster wins, the caster may automatically do one of the following once per game:

· Kill a single character (a Notable or an NPC but not a Major Foe).

· Find 100 Gold.

· Find a Grimoire with 4 spells of your choice.

· Steal any single Special Item from another character.

· Increase a single Attribute of the caster by 1 for the duration of 2 weeks.

· Decrease by 1 a single Attribute of another Notable for the duration of 1 week.

· Have a single Notable fall in love with the caster, with no regards for gender, sexual preferences, age or Status. After one week, the victim breaks away from the spell and will NEVER fall in love again with the caster. After the experience, the victim will HATE the caster.

A caster reduced to 0 Mind by a confrontation with the demon becomes a babbling idiot and is no longer able to cast spells, read or complete any Milestones. The caster regains these abilities if the caster's Mind score is healed. A caster reduced to 0 Will will no longer be capable of resisting urges and passions. After 2d6 days, the caster will become a homeless drunkard. A caster reduced to 0 Charisma will no longer be able to have meaningful interactions with other humans, and will go to live in the forest, succumbing to the harsh conditions of life d6 weeks later.

Actions

• 53-54 Scourge of the Dead

Cast this spell to avoid an encounter with undead creatures (Wanton Vampire, Swamp Undead and Terrifying Skeletons) or to gain Advantage on all rolls vs. the Graveyard Guardian.

• 55-56-61-62 Witch's Flight

To cast this spell, the caster must first play the Raid the Graveyard and Search for Rare Herbs actions to find ingredients. Once the ingredients are found, the spell may be cast. The caster smears his/her body with a mixture of hallucinogens and fat from a human corpse and gains the power to fly for a short period, riding a broomstick. This lets the caster flee any single encounter without suffering any consequences, or return home automatically after getting lost in the forest. A character who is seen flying on a broomstick will automatically be accused of witchcraft and be put on trial by the Inquisition.

• 63-64-65-66 Witch's Ladder

The caster creates a string of cord or wool, with many knots and feathers, to curse a person. If the witch's ladder is hidden in the person's house, under the person's bed, the person will die after a number of weeks equal to the sum of the person's Vigor and Will. The curse stops if the caster dies or if the witch's ladder is found (this is equal to discovering a Secret, and requires spending 3 Clues) and brought to church. The caster may hide the Witch's Ladder under the bed of a character with a successful Dexterity roll

vs. the victim's Alertness. If the roll is unsuccessful, the caster will be caught and automatically be Suspected of witchcraft.

Actions

During the game, your character will perform Actions from the following list. You play using a planner (which should include date and day of the week) and you note the character's action on the page. When you play a scene with a Contact and you want to control that character instead of the character you are currently playing, you SWITCH to that character. Imagine you are the director of a TV serial and you move from a character to another. When you Switch, the previous character fades in the background, but you can Switch back on that character later in the story. You must stay with a character a minimum of 1 day/1 action before switching to another. All characters are connected, so you could eventually play everyone, or stay most of the time on a single character if that's what you prefer. All characters have unique abilities, weaknesses, and goals. You will learn them as you play.

Unless otherwise indicated, an action takes 1 day (advance the calendar by 1 day). Of course, this doesn't mean the character spent one full day performing the action. The characters are assumed to go on with their daily life, full of obligations with work, family, church, and so on. Certain actions can be attempted only on specific days of the week. For example, the general market is open only on Wednesdays, so you may play the General Market Action only on a Wednesday. Certain actions are connected to seasons, e.g., you may pick mushrooms only from April to November.

Some actions are Illegal – once you perform them, the character has a Secret. If this is discovered, the character may be accused of various crimes, suspected of witchcraft, and so on. The consequences may lead to excommunication, being cast out of the village, imprisonment or even death.You plan your action for the day and then you roll to determine when the next Event takes place. Roll d6. This is the day the new Event will happen (if you roll a 1, the event happens today). Note that certain events may prevent you from completing an action.

Actions

For example, you planned to Pick Mushrooms but an edict is issued: nobody can visit the forest on odd days. Today it's May 13, so you can't pick mushrooms.

Accuse

If your character has proof that someone is a witch or has killed someone or stolen something, you may denounce them to the authorities, and gain 4d6 Gold for your service. You may play the Trial or assume that the person is jailed (for theft) or put to death (for witchcraft or assassination).

Assassination (Illegal)

You plan to kill someone, either one of the Notables or someone you met during some Event. You can try to do it yourself or hire an assassin.

DIY Assassination: To do it yourself, you must Test Will vs.1 to find the courage, then Dexterity vs. the victim's Alertness to skulk on the target. If the target is higher Status than you, you must also Test Mind or Charisma vs. the victim's Status to be able to meet the target. Once this is done, Test Dexterity or Vigor vs. the victim's Vigor. If all these rolls are successful, you kill the target and gain a Secret (you are an assassin).

If any of your rolls fail, you may try again after 2d6 days.

If the Dexterity vs. Alertness "skulking" roll fails, the victim is alerted and calls Guards (Danger 23). Immediately test Dexterity vs. the Guards' Alertness. If you succeed, you manage to escape. If you fail, you must fight the Guards.

If your Dexterity or Vigor roll fails, you fail to kill the victim. The victim will first defend themselves (fight a Combat encounter, but you will have Disadvantage on your first die) and then call Guards (repeat the procedure described above).

Hiring a Professional: You must first roll Mind vs. 2 to find someone to do the dirty work. Pay the assassin 25 Gold per point of Status possessed by the victim, counting Status 0 as 1. Assassinating a Status 0-1 person will cost you 25 Gold, assassinating a Status 2 person will cost you 50 Gold, and so on. You then switch to the profile of the Charming Assassin (Danger 16) and use that to perform the rolls above, but you have 3 rerolls that you can use for any dice during the assassination mission. If the assassin is caught, the assassin will accuse you. Repeat the Guard encounter procedure explained above. If they catch the Assassin, you will be Tortured (Test Will vs. 2; on a failure, you will confess and be put to death in 2d6 days. On a success, you can test Mind or Charisma vs. 2 to turn a death penalty into the Jailed condition).

Assassinating one of your Contacts is easier. If you involve the Contact in any scene with you, you just need to test Will to summon up the courage and then Vigor or Dexterity to kill the person. The Will test is vs. 2 if the person is a friend and vs. 4 if he/she is someone you Love. The victim is automatically caught off guard: you don't need any roll to skulk.

If you have a dose of poison, you can kill someone without the Vigor/Dexterity test. You just need to share a Social Event with that character.

If you kill someone, advance the Event Track by d6. If you kill someone you Love, advance it by 2d6.

Attend Social Event

Social events like festivals are often open to the whole population. Some may be restricted by Status (the commoners from the streets will not be invited to the Countess' birthday). In a Social Event, you may contact and try to Befriend, Seduce or engage in Social Combat any Notable.

Attend Sunday Mass (Sundays only)

All characters are supposed to attend mass at Church on Sundays. The only people who are exempt from this are Jailed characters, characters who are sick in bed, known/suspected witches, and Jewish people. It's a Social Event and you may Befriend, Court or engage in Social Combat any Notable. Attending Mass can also break some curses from witches. With a donation of 5 Gold, you may gain 1 vial of Holy Water.

Actions

Befriend Someone

At any Social Event, you may attempt to become friends with any character of the same Status or lower. This requires a successful Charisma test vs. 1. You may not become friends with someone who is your Enemy (as per your Contacts). If you roll a 1 on the attempt to Befriend, the person will become your Enemy instead.

To Befriend someone of higher Status than you, subtract the difference in Status from your roll. For example, if you are Status 1 and want to befriend a Status 3 person, test at -2.

Blackmail (illegal)

Once you know someone's Secret, you may blackmail that person, extorting from them an amount of Gold equal to 3 times their Status (minimum 3 Gold). You may blackmail a person a maximum of 3 times per every Secret you discover about that person. The person is now your Enemy.

If you are accused and judged guilty of Blackmailing, you must pay a compensation of five times what you gained from blackmailing.

Black Market (illegal)

You try to buy something illegal, like Grimoires, secret information or poison, or rare, like a bestiary. To start, you must test Mind roll vs. 1 to locate someone willing to sell. On a roll of 1, you ask the wrong person and become Suspected of Witchcraft. If you are already Suspected, Guards will come (play Danger 23). On a failure, you can try again after d6+3 days. On a success, you locate someone willing to sell a Grimoire, Poison, a Bestiary or Secret Information.

The content of Grimoires is always random. You can't request a Grimoire containing specific spells. See the Spells section for details. The cost of a Grimoire will be 30 Gold +10 Gold per spell contained in it.

A Bestiary is a book explaining everything about beasts. It takes 6-Mind days to read it and it costs 15 Gold.

A vial of Poison strong enough to kill an adult person of Vigor 1 will cost 30 Gold. 60 Gold will buy a dose strong enough to kill a person of Vigor 2, and 90 Gold will buy a dose strong enough to kill any person. Use the same procedure for a Grimoire, but on a 1, Guards come and try to catch you.

You may try to buy Secret Information about a specific Notable. You can buy 1 Clue, at a cost of 5 Gold times the Status of the target. 3 Clues will typically unlock that person's Secret. After acquiring 1 Clue, the character can try again to visit the Black Market after d6 days. Clues bought for a specific person may not be used to buy any other Secret in the game. The procedure for buying 1 Clue is the same as above. On a roll of 1, the target of your investigation is informed of your asking, and is now your Enemy.

To purchase other things, see also Buy and General Market, below.

Buy

Characters are assumed to provide for their daily needs, food and clothing. The game zooms in only on purchases that are relevant to the plot of the story or out of the ordinary.

This is a list of things that is possible to buy everyday. For more unusual things, you should go to the general market, which happens only on Wednesdays, where there is more competition and prices can be a little lower. For forbidden things like Grimoires, see Black Market, above.

A Bottle of Fine Wine: 9 Gold. Useful in many occasions as a bribe.

A Delicacy: 4 Gold. Useful to bribe gluttonous men and ravenous creatures.

A Prestigious Gift: The cost is 5 Gold times the receiver's Status. For example, a Gift appropriate for a Status 3 person will cost 15 Gold. This will give you Advantage on a single Charisma roll with the person

Actions

receiving the Gift. If you give multiple Gifts to the same person in a period of a month, to keep enjoying the Advantage each Gift must be at least 2 Gold more expensive than the former.

An Ornate Sharp Knife: 5 Gold. You may reroll a single Combat die, but if the reroll is a 1, the Knife snaps and must be discarded.

A Small Jewel: 2 Gold x buyer's Status, with a minimum of 2. This is the minimum a man must spend to court a lady. Without such a trinket, you can't even perform your first Charisma roll.

Challenge to Duel (Illegal)

You may challenge to duel only a character who is the same Status as you, or lower. To see if your target accepts the challenge, roll your Charisma vs. the target's Will. On a failure, the target will find an excuse or otherwise refuse to fight. On a success, you can continue the following procedure. Organizing the duel will take d6 days. Dueling is illegal and doing it without being caught requires some planning. At the end of the preparation period, roll Mind vs. 2. On a failure, Guards (Danger 23) will come and interrupt the duel, and fine you (5 Gold times your Status, with a minimum of 5). If you do not pay, they will try to catch you and put you in Jail. If the Guards do not show up, you may conduct the duel, performing a Combat with your target.

Court

You look for a companion, ideally to get married and raise a family. A man looking for a woman should present her with a gift (either A Small Jewel or a Prestigious Gift) and in general be of the same Status or higher. Women can attract men without offering them gifts. The first problem is meeting candidates: you can only court your Contacts, or anyone who is present at a social event, like Mass on Sundays. Some events from the Events Track will give you the opportunity to meet other people.

Courtship happens in 3 phases, each requiring a week of time. At the end of each week, test Charisma vs. the target's Will. A failure means a setback - the week is lost, but the courtship can continue. If three Charisma failures in a row are rolled, that person is not interested and you may not roll again - take him/her out of your mind. If the third roll in a row is successful, the characters become engaged.

Marriage: After d3 months of engagement, you are supposed to marry. Marriage requires an expenditure of 10 times your Status, in Gold. Use the higher Status in the couple to calculate these expenses. You are allowed to marry later if you don't have the necessary Gold - there will be a bit of questions and peer pressure, but people will understand if you wait because you do not have money. Check the Calendar section because during certain holidays it is not possible to have weddings.

A marriage is a Social Event that involves all contacts (including Enemies!) of the couple. All will be present and bring gifts. You may move any Special Items from the characters who are invited to the couple, or Status x 5 Gold (using the lower Status of the guest or the couple) if the guests have nothing of interest.

Gather Firewood

Anyone can go to the forest and gather some firewood to resell at the next General Market. It takes two days to gather enough firewood that can be sold for 1 Gold. In winter months, you need three days to collect enough firewood for 1 Gold. Every day you spend collecting firewood, roll d6. On a 1, you have an encounter. Roll d6 on this list:

1) You meet Kendrick the Woodcutter (Character 33). You may interact with him as in a social event.
2) Bear, Danger 13
3) Boar, Danger 15
4) You see a Hare. You may catch it if you succeed an Alertness roll vs. 2 and then a Dexterity roll vs. 3. The Hare can be kept as a bribe or sold for 1 Gold.
5) Slumber mushrooms, Danger 46
6) Whispers in the Forest, Danger 62.

General Market (Wednesdays only)

On Wednesday, a general market is held in the main square and vendors from nearby cottages and other villages come to sell all manners of wares. Visiting the market, you can buy the following items:

An Amulet: 6 Gold. They say it can bring good luck.

Actions

A Bottle of Fine Wine: 8 Gold. Useful in many occasions as a bribe.

A Bunch of Garlic Flowers: 1 Gold. Available only in the months of June to September. It may be useful against vampires, but maybe it's just a myth.

A Bunch of Roses: 2 Gold. Giving this together with a Small Jewel or Prestigious Gift, you may reroll any die that rolled a 1 on the Charisma roll. Not available in Winter.

A Bunch of Rue: 1 Gold. This may be useful to catch a basilisk. Available only in May and June.

A Bunch of Wolvesbane: 1 Gold. This may give you some protection from werewolves and can be used to create poison. Available only in the months of June, July, August.

A Delicacy: 4 Gold. Useful to bribe gluttonous men and ravenous creatures.

A Fancy Hat: 5 Gold. Useful to look stylish.

A Fine Pair of Shoes: 8 Gold. When you run away from combat, you may reroll a single die.

A Good Cape: 6 Gold. It will protect you from inclement weather.

A Good Helmet: 20 Gold. The helmet protects your head and lets you reroll a roll on the Death Table, once per game.

A Heavy Mace: 8 Gold. Useful to destroy the Terrifying Skeletons that haunt the swamp.

A Heavy Flail: 8 Gold. This weapon lets you reroll a failed Combat roll. However, if the reroll is a 1, you wound yourself and lose 1 Vigor or 1 Dexterity (your choice)

A Jar of Honey: 2 Gold. Useful to distract bears.

A Lamb: 4 Gold. Useful to satiate the appetite of certain monsters.

A Loyal Dog: 4 Gold. Useful to hunt and to fight rats.

A Pair of Fancy Gloves: 6 Gold. They say they may be useful to scare off fairies.

A Prestigious Gift: The cost is 5 Gold times the receiver's Status. For example, a Gift appropriate for a Status 3 person will cost 15 Gold. This will give you Advantage on a single Charisma roll with the person receiving the Gift. If you give multiple Gifts to the same person in a period of a month, to keep enjoying the Advantage each Gift must be at least 2 Gold more expensive than the former.

A Set of Lockpicks: 20 Gold. They may be required to open a locked door.

A Sharp Knife: 4 Gold. You may reroll a single Combat die, but if the reroll is a 1, the Knife snaps and must be discarded.

A Small Jewel: 2 Gold x buyer's Status. This is the minimum a man should spend to court a lady. Without such a trinket, you can't even perform your first Charisma roll.

A Splendid Housecat: 4 Gold. Having a cat around is an efficient protection against vermin and certain goblins.

A Sturdy Shield: 6 Gold. If you pass a Test of Dexterity vs. your foe's Dexterity, you may Sacrifice the Shield to avoid losing 1 Vigor in a combat encounter. If the test is not passed, the shield survives to be used in another combat encounter.

A Weasel: 7 Gold. Useful to hunt basilisks and to fight rat infestation. If you have a weasel, you may not have other pets.

A Wooden Stake: 1 Gold. Useful to fight vampires, it gives you 2 rerolls in combat against these beasts.

Gossip

You spend the day gossiping about someone and trying to learn their secrets. You may perform a Mind roll vs.2 to pick up some information about a Notable. On a success, you gain 1 Clue that you may use **only** to offset the cost of revealing a Secret of that person. However, if you roll a 1, that person will be informed that you are asking nosy questions about them, and will now be considered your Enemy.

Hunt

You brave the wilderness to look for some creature or wanted man who has been plaguing the area. Whom you can hunt depends on Events or on the season. In general, finding someone or some creature, if the character's description does not say otherwise, will require spending 2 Clues. In a day of hunting, you can generate 1 Clue that may be spent for that only, by passing an Alertness roll vs. your target's Mind or Dexterity (the best of the two). This means that, in the best cases, you can find an average target in 2 days minimum. **If you have a Loyal Dog you roll TWICE per day.**

Some creatures, like the tatzelwurm, the basilisk or the swamp drake, are seen rarely. You may Hunt them only when an Event allows to do so (there will be an event saying that the creature has been sighted). During Summer, you may hunt the Guardian of Wheat. During Winter, you may hunt Jack Frost. During Autumn, you may hunt Jack o'Lantern. During Spring, you may hunt animals. When you roll a 1 on your Alertness roll, you fail to generate any Clues and must roll d6 and face the appropriate Danger:

1) Ravens, Danger 45
2) Bear, Danger 13
3) Boar, Danger 15
4) Pagans, Danger 44
5) Slumber Mushrooms, Danger 46
6) Wolves, Danger 66.

Investigate

This is a generic Action that you choose when an Event gives you the option to Investigate some mystery. This normally means you will have to play a Scene, as told by the Event.

When you Investigate the main enemy (to discover who is the Main Foe threatening Eldritchwood), you must first generate Clues. Test your Mind or Alertness (your choice) vs. 2. On a success, you generate 1 Clue. On a failure, you just waste a day chasing wrong leads. On a roll of 1, you end up in trouble: roll d66 to select a random Danger and play it. Once you have

Clues, you may spend 2 Clues to roll d6 on the list of Major Foes. The Foe you roll is NOT the final enemy of the game. By playing this action multiple times, you can reduce the number of suspects until you know for sure who the Main Foe is.

Example: You must understand who killed a drunkard in a dark alley. You generate 2 Clues and roll on the Major Foes list. The result is the Whispering Queen. Now you know that the Whispering Queen has NOTHING to do with the killing. After some time, you put together 2 more Clues and roll again. You already have excluded the Queen, so if you roll her, you reroll until you select a different suspect.

Clues generated by a character can be passed onto a contact of that character, playing the Visit a Friend action. This is a smart way to use different characters for different "jobs". E.g., *you could use a smart character to pick up Clues and then a fighting character to attack the Main Foe.*

Pick Mushrooms (April to November)

You may look for edible mushrooms from April to November. Test Alertness vs. 1. On a success, you find enough mushrooms that you can sell for 1 Gold. On a failure, the day is unfruitful. On a roll of 1, you have an unpleasant encounter. Roll d6:

1) Mischievous Fairy, Danger 35
2) Bear, Danger 13
3) Boar, Danger 15
4) Pagans, Danger 44
5) Slumber mushrooms, Danger 46
6) Whispers in the Forest, Danger 62.

Raid the Graveyard (Illegal)

In some cases, casting spells may require acquiring parts of dead bodies. The only way to obtain some is to skulk into the graveyard at night. To get into the graveyard you need either to pick the lock of the gate (you need a set of lockpicks) with a successful Dexterity roll vs. 2, or to climb the wall (with a successful Dexterity roll vs. 3). When picking locks, on a 1 you break your tools. On a failure, nothing happens and you can try again. When climbing, a 1 means you fall and lose 1 Vigor or 1 Dexterity. Once you are in, you must avoid detection by the Graveyard Guardian (Danger 24), rolling a successful Dexterity vs. his Alertness. If you succeed, you may steal what you came to steal, or steal some decorative objects from graves for a total of 2d6 Gold. If you fail, follow the rules explained in the description of Danger 24.

Resting

Some times, you will have to rest to recover from a disease or to let your wounds heal. During days where you rest, you may only Read or Pray. Any other action is too strenuous for the day to count as rest. One lost point of Vigor or Dexterity heals in five days. Other conditions have the number of days of rest required to recover in their description.

If events happen while you are resting, unless the event happens specifically to you in your house, you may Switch to another character (one of your Contacts, or a character affected by the Event as per the Event's description). At the end of the rest period, you may continue to play that character or switch back to the resting character.

Pray

You spend the day in prayer, at the Church, at a small shrine, or in the privacy of your home. This may be required to break a curse or as a preparation for a spell. If you pray for a full week, with no interruption from Events (you either ignore the Events or manage not to roll any), you gain 1 universal reroll. The "Pray" action is available to all characters except witches – they can spend time in church paying lip service, but this has no effect.

Read

You spend time reading a book. Depending on the content, reading a book will require a variable number of days. For Grimoires, the time needed is 2d6 days minus your Mind Attribute, per spell. You do not have to read all the content of a book in one go, you can take breaks and read more later. Days spent reading are not "wasted" if you are interrupted. If an event destroys your book before you can complete reading it, you will still partially enjoy the benefits of the portion you read. For example, if you have a Grimoire with 4 spells, read 3 spells and then the book is

destroyed, you still have learned the 3 spells you have studied.

Reading a Bestiary requires 6 - Mind days.

Rescue from Prison

When a character is imprisoned, the character's contacts may play a Rescue action, even pooling their resources to bribe the character out of jail. This will require a successful Charisma test vs. 3 and the expenditure of 10 times the character's Status, in Gold. If the character has been jailed for a serious crime (witchcraft, assassination, theft of over 30 Gold) or has been sentenced to death, the Charisma test is rolled with Disadvantage and the bribe amount is tripled. On a roll of 1 on the Charisma test, the character attempting the bribe is jailed, too. On a failure, the bribe is simply not possible, but another character may try again d3 days later, increasing the bribe by 25% (round up).

Search for herbs

You go into the woods looking for healing herbs. Roll Alertness vs. 1. On a success, you find what you were looking for. On a failure, nothing happens and you return home empty-handed. On a roll of 1, you Roll d6 on this list and face the appropriate Danger:

1) Ravens, Danger 45. If the date is 20 to 25th December, you encounter the Krampus instead (Danger 69).
2) Bear, Danger 13. During winter, you meet Jack Frost (Danger 25) instead.
3) Boar, Danger 15; in October or November, you meet Jack o'Lantern instead, Danger 26.
4) Pagans, Danger 44. If you already know that the Major Foe is the Beast of Eldritchwood, you meet a Wandering Werewolf instead (Danger 65)
5) Slumber Mushrooms, Danger 46. If you know that the Major Foe is the Swamp Witch, play Danger 53.
6) Wolves, Danger 66.

Sell Stolen Goods (Illegal)

You may sell any ill-gotten gains for their full value with a successful Charisma or Mind (use the best) test vs. 1. On a failure, you find no buyer. You can try again after 1d6 days. On a roll of 1, play Danger 23.

Actions

Stroll through the Forest

You go through the forest for a walk, trying to ease your worried mind. Roll a d6. On a 1, you have an encounter. Roll on the following list:

1) Mischievous Fairy, Danger 35
2) Bear, Danger 13
3) Boar, Danger 15
4) Roll a die: 1-3 Lizbeth the herbalist (character 46), 4-6 Erania the forest lady (character 62)
5) a Bandit (Danger 11)
6) The encounter depends on the season. In Winter, you meet Jack Frost (Danger 25); in Autumn, you meet a Jack O'Lantern (Danger 26); on the seven days before Christmas, you meet the Krampus (Danger 69); In Summer, you meet the Guardian of Wheat (Danger 73); in Spring, you meet the Dust (Danger 68).

Theft (Illegal)

You plan to steal some valuables! The objects will come from the possession of someone who is Status 2 or 3. Choose a value of 10, 20 or 30 Gold. You must roll a successful Mind roll to conceive a plan, and then a Dexterity roll to steal and avoid detection. The rolls are vs. 1 if you try to steal 10 Gold, vs. 2 if you try to steal 20 Gold, and vs.3 if you try to steal 30 Gold. If the Mind roll fails, you may try again after 1 week. If you fail the Dexterity roll, play an encounter with Guards (Danger 23). This event lets you play a generic theft: feel free to invent the details of the object stolen, as long as it is recognizable (it can't be just coins, it must be an item like a work of art or a jewel) and of the appropriate monetary value. You may also attempt to steal any Special Item from another Notable you have played during the current game.

When you steal something, your crime is a Secret that can be revealed by events or other character's actions in the game. If the Secret is revealed, the original possessor of the item becomes your enemy.

Use Trait

You use a trait or an ability that is listed on your character's profile. *For example, Frey the butcher is drunk and his daughter Jehanne, the acting character,* *decides to use her One Apple a Day ability to have him sober up.* The use of some abilities is automatic, or may require a die roll: refer to your character profile for more information.

Visit the Apothecary

You may perform this action to go buy a cure for a disease from Moishe the Apothecary (Character 25), for the price of 10 Gold (5 Gold if you are Moishe).

Visit a Friend

You may just perform this Action to meet one of your Contacts. This can be useful to switch to that character (that is, you stop playing the current character and start playing your friend). When you visit a friend, you may lend to that character any Special Item you have, or up to 50 Gold, but if the character receiving money has lower Status than the character giving money, you must spend 1 Fate. Money given to friends should be returned within 3 months. If this does not happen, the friend owing money loses 1 Status until the debt is paid back in full. You may also use this action TO BE VISITED by a contact, for example when you are resting at home.

Visit the Goldsmith

Play this action to go to sell some piece of jewelry or have jewelry made for you from Venceslaus the goldsmith (Character 12).

Visit the Herbalist

You may perform this action to go buy a cure for a disease from Lizbeth the herbalist (Character 46) for 5 Gold (free if you are Lizbeth or if you are in a love relationship with Lizbeth).

Visit the Moneylender

You may visit a moneylender and borrow up to 50 Gold. Choose how much money you want to borrow, then play Danger 36. Do not read Danger 36 until you have decided how much you are going to borrow. You may not borrow money if you already owe money.

Actions

Visit the Tavern

You may visit the Tavern to drink (spend 2 Gold, roll d6; on a 6, you gain 1 Clue; once you have gathered a total of 2 Clues, you cannot get Clues from the Tavern anymore) or to gamble. To gamble, choose how much Gold you want to wager, up to 20. Roll a d6. On a 1, you lose all and are accused of cheating (play Danger 21). On a 2-3, you lose your money. On a 4-6, you win double your ante. Keep track of how much money you win by gambling. If you win more than 30 Gold, roll a 1 in 6 chance of an encounter with a robber (Danger 61) on your way home.

The Notables

The Notables are the most important characters in Eldritchwood. It's a diverse cast. You will learn to know them well only over the course of several games. The various characters are NOT balanced or equivalent: each of them has unique characteristics that may give you advantages or disadvantages in different moments of the game. Some have a better social standing, some begin the game with more Gold, some have better attributes than others, and some belong to marginalized groups, just like in real life.

All characters have a corresponding number from 11 to 66. When you begin play, DO NOT READ the characters' description. Just roll d66 and select the corresponding character. This is where your "camera" is set at the beginning of your story. Let the story begin by playing that character. You decide if she/he is going to be a protagonist or not. As soon as you meet another character, for example by playing the Visit a Friend action, you can switch to that character. You do not have to play a character you don't like for more than a day or two: that character is simply the introduction to the story. Most characters get a chance to interact with each other during social events. For example, most characters (excluding known witches and Moishe the Apothecary, who is Jewish) meet each other in Church on Sundays, during mass.

If you want to create your own character (a traveler passing through Eldritchwood as the supernatural events begin), the rules are at the end of the list of Notables.

If the rules ask you to meet a random character, roll d66 again and meet the corresponding character. Obviously, you cannot meet yourself or a character who is no longer in play, so roll again if the d66 selects your character or a dead character.

All characters have a list of contacts, with different relationships such as friendship, love, and enmities. These have a bearing on the game.

You are not required to continue playing the same character throughout the game, but you can do so if you want. Using the talents of multiple, different characters with different training and equipment is your best bet to defeat the supernatural menace that is threatening the good folks of Eldritchwood.

The Notables

11

Name	Gold	Status
Lady Elianna of Eldritchwood	40	3

Vigor	Dexterity	Mind	Charisma	Will	Alertness
1	1	2	3	2	1

Milestones

- Marry a Status 3+ man, gain Status +1. If the man dies or the marriage causes Scandal, lose the bonus. You may not marry again sooner than d6 months later. If the marriage was True Love, you may not remarry during this game.
- Find True Love with a man with minimum Vigor 2, Charisma 2, Mind 2 and Status 2.
- Collect 3 Grimoires to gain +1 Will and 1 random spell. Collect 6 Grimoires to gain +1 Mind.
- Survive 2 combat encounters to gain +1 Dexterity.
- Gain 2 Charisma rerolls if you win any social conflict with another notable of Status 2+.

Traits

Determined: You have 3 universal rerolls that you may use on any type of conflicts.

Expensive jewelry: Sell them to gain 30 Gold. Selling takes time: you will finalize the sale and receive the money 2d6 days later. If you sell them, roll a 2 in 6 chance of a theft attempt (roll Alertness vs. Dexterity 2 of a common thief to prevent the theft). If the jewels are stolen, a character may find their location by spending 3 Clues and recover them by fighting a Violent Robber (Danger 61). The jewels are a target for theft and may be stolen by other characters.

Contacts

Your jewels were fashioned by Venceslaus the goldsmith (character 12), who gave you a special price because he owed your father a favor. You may convince Venceslaus to go after your jewels if they are stolen by a successful test of a Charisma vs. his Will.

Eleanor (character 22) is your enemy.

Yolanda (character 36) is your friend.

The Notables

12

Name	Gold	Status
Venceslaus the goldsmith	30	2

Vigor	Dexterity	Mind	Charisma	Will	Alertness
2	1	1	1	2	1

Milestones

- Marry a Status 3 woman, gain Status +1. If the woman dies or the marriage causes Scandal, lose the bonus. You may not marry again sooner than d6 months later.
- Find True Love by marrying Lizbeth the herbalist. If you find True Love, gain +1 to one attribute of your choice and 3 universal rerolls.
- Collect 100 Gold to gain +1 Status.
- Collect 3 Grimoires to gain 1 spell of your choice.
- Survive 3 combats to gain +1 Alertness.
- Gain 10 Gold if you sell an important piece of jewelry.

Traits

Obese: You may not use rerolls when fleeing, chasing someone, climbing or performing any actions of Dexterity or Vigor, including combat encounters.

Create jewelry: Spend 10 Gold and 10 days to create a piece that can be sold for 20 Gold. Sell it to someone with a successful Charisma vs. Will roll. You will receive the money d6 days later. Roll a 2 in 6 chance of a theft attempt (test Alertness vs. Dexterity 2 of a common thief to prevent the theft) one day before the sale. If the jewel is stolen, a character may find it by spending 3 Clues and fighting a Violent Robber (Danger 61).

Contacts

You owe your fortune to Elianna's family (character 11).

You are in love with Lizbeth the herbalist (character 46). If you marry her, you complete your True Love milestone. But this is Unrequited Love. You need to succeed at your Charisma vs. Will test three times for Lizbeth to accept your love.

You are on bad terms with Kendrick the woodcutter (character 33) and with Frey the butcher (character 24) whom you consider unrefined and vulgar.

13

Name	Gold	Status
Hildegardis the Wise	10	1

Vigor	Dexterity	Mind	Charisma	Will	Alertness
1	1	2	1	2	1

Milestones

- Discover the cause of the fire that killed your wife and sons to gain 1 Fate point. This is a Secret and requires the expenditure of 5 Clues. Feel free to invent the story details once you have enough Clues. If you need a character to be responsible for the fire, select a random Notable or a random Danger (your choice of which) which you may then confront.
- Collect 3 white Grimoires to gain 1 extra white spell of your choice.
- Spend 15 Gold on a special diet and treatment to gain +1 Vigor. You may do this only once per game.

Traits

<u>Determined</u>: You have 2 universal rerolls.
<u>Investigative Mind</u>: You have 3 rerolls on Mind rolls.
<u>Strong Willed</u>: You have Advantage on all Will rolls. If another character is trying to persuade Hildegardis, that character has Disadvantage.

Contacts

Your wife and two adult sons died in a fire several years ago, so you are left without any family. You managed to rebuild your house. You are still investigating to understand how it happened. You are a friend of Moishe (character 25) and Crisanta (character 61).

The Notables

Name	Gold	Status
Jehanne, butcher's daughter	5	0

Vigor	Dexterity	Mind	Charisma	Will	Alertness
2	1	1	2	1	2

Milestones

- Find True Love with Ward (character 35). Gain +4 universal rerolls and 1 Fate if this happens.
- Collect 50 Gold to start a business and gain +1 Status. Collect 100 Gold to gain another +1 Status.
- Collect 3 Grimoires to gain 1 spell.
- Survive 4 combat encounters to gain +1 Vigor.

Traits

Healthy Country Girl: You may reroll any Vigor roll to avoid or shake off a disease.

One Apple A Day: You may remove one Condition from yourself or from another character. You may use this ability once per month.

Contacts

You are the only daughter of Frey the butcher (character 24) and grow under his strict disciplinarian control. Despite his stern ways, you love him. If you want to participate in any social events, you must win a test of Charisma vs. Frey's Will.

You are friend of Ilinn (character 42) and Matthew (character 66).

You have a crush on Ward (character 35).

The Notables

Name			Gold		Status
Percival Quickfingers			15		0
Vigor	Dexterity	Mind	Charisma	Will	Alertness
1	3	2	1	1	2

Milestones

- Find True Love with a woman with Mind 2+ and Status 1+ to gain 10 Gold and 3 rerolls.
- Collect 20 Gold to gain +1 Alertness or Mind.
- Steal Precious Jewels to gain 25 Gold.
- Win 3 combats to gain +1 Vigor.
- Challenge Amari to a duel and defeat him to gain 3 universal rerolls.
- Gain 2 Dexterity/Alertness rerolls every time you escape or avoid capture by Guards (Danger 23).
-

Traits

<u>Lockpicks</u>: You have 3 rerolls that you may use to open doors or locked chests.
<u>Hidden Dagger</u>: Once per game, wound one character automatically.
<u>Stealth</u>: You have 2 rerolls on Dexterity vs. Alertness conflicts to avoid being heard or seen.
<u>Ill-gotten Gains</u>: Once per week, you may roll Dexterity vs. a number of your choice. If you succeed, you gain an amount of Gold equal to that number. If you roll a 1, however, you must roll an Alertness roll vs. 2 or be Jailed.

Contacts

Ward (character 35) and Amari (character 23) are your enemies. You have a trade relationship with Oswald the blacksmith (character 21) who sometimes creates daggers, keys and lockpicks for you.

The Notables

Name	Gold	Status
Vendaya the dyer	2	0

Vigor	Dexterity	Mind	Charisma	Will	Alertness
1	1	2	1	2	3

Milestones

- Collect 10 Gold to gain 1 universal reroll.
- Collect 3 Grimoires to gain 1 random spell.
- Survive 4 combat encounters to gain +1 Vigor.
- Spend 8 Gold on a special diet and treatment to gain +1 Vigor. The bonus is lost after 2 weeks, but the diet and treatment can be continued if you have the Gold to spare.
- Collect 30 Gold to gain 1 Fate.

Traits

Determined: You start the game with 4 universal rerolls.

Inquisitive: Once at the end of every week, you can roll Alertness vs. the Mind of any character that you have contacted during that week. On a failure, nothing happens. On a success, you gain 1 Clue that you can spend ONLY to offset the cost of that person's Secret, if any.

Contacts

You are a widow: your husband died after an unsuccessful medical treatment by Crisanta (character 61). Now you blame her for his death. Crisanta is your enemy.

You have a professional relationship with Aelfric the greengrocer (character 63) and Millard the miller (character 31). Harold, a retired soldier who was a friend of her late husband (character 52) is your friend.

The Notables

Name	Gold	Status	
Oswald the Blacksmith	20	1	

Vigor	Dexterity	Mind	Charisma	Will	Alertness
3	1	1	1	2	2

Milestones

- Marry a Status 2+ woman, gain Status +1. If the woman dies or the marriage causes Scandal, lose the bonus. You may not marry again sooner than d6 months later. If the marriage was True Love, you may not remarry during this game.
- Find True Love with a woman with minimum Charisma 2, Mind 1 and Status 2.
- Spend 100 Gold to gain +1 Status.
- Collect 3 Grimoires of any color to gain 1 random spell of a random color.
- Survive 5 combat encounters to gain 3 Vigor rerolls.

Traits

Blacksmith: You are a skilled blacksmith and can create a multitude of objects out of iron. If the rules do not say otherwise, the creation of any item takes 1 day. You may create a Key, a Sharp Knife, a set of Lockpicks, a Helmet, a Horseshoe.

Strong: You may reroll any failed Vigor roll once.

Contacts

You are the secret lover of Eleanor the silk trader (character 22) but this relationship is unknown to your or her friends (it's a Secret). You have a trade relationship with Percival Quickfingers (character 15) and are a frequent customer of Wilburn the baker (character 34). You are a friend of Millard the miller (character 31), Moishe the apothecary (character 25), Amari the mercenary (character 23) and Erania the forest lady (character 62).

22

Name	Gold	Status
Eleanor the silk-trader	30	2

Vigor	Dexterity	Mind	Charisma	Will	Alertness
1	1	2	2	1	2

Milestones

- Marry Oswald the blacksmith (character 21) to gain 5 universal rerolls. Before you can do so, Oswald must become Status 2.
- Win 5 social combats to gain a permanent +1 to Mind, Charisma or Alertness (your choice).
- Survive 2 combat encounters to gain +1 to Vigor.
- Collect 3 Grimoires of any type to gain 1 random spell. The random spell may be of any color contained in any grimoire in your possession.

Traits

Sharp Tongue: You have 5 rerolls that you can use only in Social Combat.

Shut Down the Gossips: Eleanor can use this ability up to 3 times per game. When she uses this ability, no acting character may reveal a Secret in the next 1d6 days. Note that Clues can still be generated and characters may still perform the Gossip action, but Clues can't be used to reveal Secrets while this ability is in effect.

Contacts

You have a secret love relationship with Oswald the blacksmith (character 21). This relationship is a Secret. You hate Elianna (character 11): you are rivals in social matters and tease each other at social events. Your best friend is Gwendoline the swordswoman (character 45). You have a trade relationship with Vendaya (character 16) who sometimes dyes your fabrics.

23

Name		Gold	Status	
Amari the mercenary		15	0	

Vigor	Dexterity	Mind	Charisma	Will	Alertness
2	1	1	1	2	2

Milestones

- Marry a woman with Mind 2+ to gain 15 Gold.
- Find True Love by marrying Gwendoline (character 45). If this happens, gain +1 to an attribute of your choice.
- Spend 50 Gold to buy a farm and gain +1 Status.
- Win 3 combats to gain +1 Vigor.
- Win 4 combats to gain +1 Dexterity.
- Win 2 combats to gain +1 Will.
- Spend 10 Gold in private lessons to gain +1 Mind.

Traits

<u>Armor and weapons</u>: You have 6 rerolls that you may use on any combat encounter. Your equipment gives +1 to Vigor in combat. It may be sold (losing the bonus) for 30 Gold.
<u>Survivor of many battles</u>: You may reroll once on the Death Table.

Contacts

You were born in West Africa, traveled with a merchant uncle and finally settled near Eldritchwood, where you fought in some local battles and became a bodyguard and mercenary. You are enemy of Percival Quickfingers (character 15). You love Gwendoline (character 45). Your friends are Oswald the blacksmith (character 21) and Ward (character 35).

The Notables

Name	Gold	Status		
Frey the butcher	30	2		
Vigor	Dexterity	Mind	Charisma	Will	Alertness
2	1	1	1	2	2

Milestones

- Marry a Status 2+ woman, gain Status +1. If the woman dies or the marriage causes Scandal, lose the bonus. You may not marry again sooner than d6 months later. If the marriage was True Love, you may not remarry during this game.
- Find True Love with a woman with minimum Charisma 2, Mind 2 and Status 2.
- Collect 100 Gold to gain +1 Fate.
- Collect 3 Grimoires to gain 1 random spell.
- Win 4 combats to gain +1 Vigor.

Traits

Large Knives: You may reroll 1 die of every combat encounter. If your knife breaks or is lost, you may replace it for free.

Hearty Diet: You may reroll every failed Vigor roll once per encounter/event.

Hard to Kill: Once per game, you may reroll a result on the Death Table.

Contacts

You are a widower, a tough man working all the time and going home always late at night. You are the stern father of Jehanne (character 14). You dislike Venceslaus the goldsmith (character 12) whom you consider a showoff. You are a friend of Bernard the cook (character 65) who sometimes fetches spices and vegetables for your meats. You are in a friendly relationship with Drustan the fishmonger (character 64) and Didimus the astrologer (character 55).

Name	Gold	Status
Moishe the apothecary	40	1

Vigor	Dexterity	Mind	Charisma	Will	Alertness
2	1	2	1	2	1

Milestones

- Find True Love with a woman with minimum Charisma 2, Mind 2 and Status 2.
- Collect 80 Gold to gain 4 universal rerolls.
- Collect 2 Grimoires to gain 1 random spell.
- Survive 4 combat encounters to gain +1 Vigor.
- Heal at least 5 people to increase Mind to 3.

Traits

<u>Jewish</u>: Due to the bias against Jewish people, you may not attend Church on Sundays. Your Status may never be higher than 2.

<u>A Cure for any ailment</u>: By spending 5 Gold in raw materials, you may find a cure for any disease except the Black Death. Any character so treated, including yourself, gets a reroll on all Vigor rolls against the disease.

Contacts

Your best friend is Hildegardis (character 13) who loves to discuss philosophy and religion with you. You are on friendly terms with Venceslaus (character 12) and have a trade relationship with Oswald the blacksmith (character 21) who sometimes fashions for you surgery blades, tweezers and other instruments. You are a friend of Millard the miller (character 31). You hate Father Cyprian (character 32).

The Notables

26

Name		Gold	Status
Ozanna		5	1

Vigor	Dexterity	Mind	Charisma	Will	Alertness
1	2	1	2	2	2

Milestones

- Find True Love with a man with minimum Vigor 2, Charisma 2 and Mind 2.
- Find True Love with a woman with minimum Mind 2. This relationship will be Secret and will cause Scandal if known due to the bias against same-sex relationships.
- Collect 50 Gold to gain +1 Will.
- Collect 3 Grimoires to gain 1 random spell.
- Survive 4 combat encounters to gain +1 Vigor.
- Gain +1 to Status to gain 3 universal rerolls.

Traits

<u>Magic Talent</u>: You may reroll any failed Mind, Will or Charisma roll for a spell to have effect or when resisting any spell effect. When reading Grimoires, your Mind counts as 1 point better.

<u>Suspected</u>: Due to the bias against foreigners, you will automatically be a Suspect in the case of an investigation by the Inquisition.

<u>Magic Knowledge</u>: Select one random spell at the beginning of the game, from a type of grimoire of your choice. You know that spell.

Contacts

You are on friendly terms with Isabelle (character 51) with whom you discuss magic (this is a dangerous Secret in game terms), Louise (character 41) and Zanda the tarot reader (character 56).

The Notables

31

Name	Gold	Status
Millard the miller	25	1

Vigor	Dexterity	Mind	Charisma	Will	Alertness
2	1	1	1	1	1

Milestones

- Collect 80 Gold to gain +1 Status.
- Collect 3 Grimoires to gain 1 random spell.
- Survive 4 combat encounters to gain +1 Vigor.
- Gain 2 Charisma rerolls if you win any social conflict with another notable of Status 1+.

Traits

A Kind Old Man: You can reroll any Charisma, Will or Mind roll once.

Shy around women: You cannot reroll any Charisma roll performed to convince or seduce women.

Military Experience: You can reroll one die in any Combat encounter.

Rat Catcher: You can reroll two dice if fighting rats.

Contacts

Your friends include Moishe the apothecary (character 25) and Percival Quickfingers (character 15). You have trade relationship with Oswald the blacksmith (character 21) and Wilburn the baker (character 34). You like Crisanta (character 61). She likes you back, but both of you are shy and there are no plans to move the relationship forwards, for the moment.

32

Name	Gold	Status
Father Cyprian	8	2

Vigor	Dexterity	Mind	Charisma	Will	Alertness
1	1	2	2	2	2

Milestones

- Offer 50 Gold to the church to gain +1 Will.
- Collect 2 Grimoires to gain 1 spell of your choice but lose 1 Mind if you do so. If Mind goes to 0 or below, you become a madman and exit the game.
- Gain 2 Charisma rerolls if you win any social conflict with another notable of Status 2+.
- Celebrate a marriage between 2 Notables to gain 1 Charisma or Alertness reroll.
- Survive being Wounded twice to gain +1 Vigor.

Traits

<u>Determined and Wise</u>: You have 3 rerolls that you may use on any type roll except combat encounters.

<u>Social Influence</u>: You may reroll once any failed Charisma roll in the game. This does not work with Jewish characters or known Witches.

<u>Cleric</u>: The Inquisition may not jail or torture you. You may involve in a scene ANY Notable except Suspected witches and Jewish people, as if they were your Contacts, but only during the Sunday mass.

Contacts

You are a friend of Ward (character 35) and Matthew the scarred boy (character 66) and enemy of Percival Quickfingers (who is a thief and a sinner). You are a father figure for the orphan Theobald (character 43) who helps you in the church.

You visit often Wilburn the baker (character 34) to buy his bread.

You are hostile towards Zanda the tarot reader (character 56), Didimus the astrologer (character 55), Crisanta (character 61) and Moishe (character 25).

33

Name	Gold	Status
Kendrick the woodcutter	8	1

Vigor	Dexterity	Mind	Charisma	Will	Alertness
2	1	1	1	2	2

Milestones

- Collect 50 Gold to gain +1 Fate.
- Collect 3 Grimoires of any color to gain 1 random spell of the same color of the last grimoire collected.
- Survive 4 combat encounters to gain +1 Vigor.
- Slay 6 Wolves, Bears or Boars (any combination) to gain the permanent ability to always reroll 2 dice in any hunting situation.
- Slay a Basilisk, Tatzelwurm, Swamp Drake to gain 1 Fate.

Traits

Forester: You may reroll once any die roll to avoid getting lost in the woods or to find your way home after getting lost. You may reroll any result on the encounter Table when performing the Stroll through the Forest action.

Axe: In all combat encounters, you may always reroll one die, unless that die rolled a 1.

Hunter: You may reroll any Alertness die to search for Clues when hunting.

Contacts

You are married to Ilinn, the baker's daughter (character 42).

You are on friendly terms with Theobald the orphan (character 43), Amari (character 23) and Didimus the astrologer (character 55).

You are on unfriendly terms with Venceslaus (character 12) because you quarreled about some wood furniture that you built for him.

The Notables

Name	Gold	Status
Wilburn the Baker	30	1

Vigor	Dexterity	Mind	Charisma	Will	Alertness
2	1	2	1	2	1

Milestones

- Find True Love with a man with minimum Charisma 1 and Mind 2. If this relationship happens, Wilburn gains 2 universal rerolls. However the relationship is considered a Secret and creates Scandal if known, due to the bias against same-sex relationships.
- Collect 50 Gold to gain +1 Status.
- Collect 3 Grimoires of any color to gain 1 random spell of random color (including a color not represented on the Grimoires in your possession).
- Survive 4 combat encounters to gain +1 Vigor.

Traits

Special Cake for You: You may slip poison or love philtres into bread, sweets etc. without arising any suspicion.

I Work at night: If you are caught going around at night, you can automatically avoid investigation, since it's normal for a baker to be working at night.

A Baker's Responsibility: If the village is struck by famine, you will be considered a Suspect.

Contacts

Your wife died of childbirth. Your daughter Ilinn (character 42) is married to Kendrick the woodcutter (character 33).

You have a trade relationship with Millard the miller (character 31), Bernard the cook (character 65), and Father Cyprian (character 32).

The Notables

Name	Gold	Status
Ward the soldier	28	1

Vigor	Dexterity	Mind	Charisma	Will	Alertness
2	1	2	2	1	1

Milestones

- Marry a Status 2+ woman, gain Status +1. If the woman dies or the marriage causes Scandal, lose the bonus. You may not marry again sooner than d6 months later. If the marriage was True Love, you may not remarry.
- Find True Love with a woman with minimum Charisma 2, Mind 2 and Status 1.
- Spend 50 Gold to buy a title and gain +1 Status.
- Win 4 combat encounters to gain +1 Vigor.
- Win 2 combat encounters to gain 1 combat reroll.

Traits

Skilled Fighter: You have 6 rerolls that you may use only on combat rolls.

Armed and Armored: You have Advantage on combat rolls. May always reroll ONCE a roll on the Death Table.

Experienced: You have 1 universal reroll.

Contacts

You are a friend of Amari (character 23). Father Cyprian (character 32) is your spiritual adviser and you may visit him (using the Visit a Friend action) to gain a +1 to your next Mind or Will roll. You must spend 1 Gold (an offer to the church) every time you do so.

You like Jehanne (Character 14) who likes you back but you consider her too young to marry. You have a Secret affair with Countess Yolanda (character 36).

You are an enemy of Percival Quickfingers (character 15).

36

Name	Gold	Status
Countess Yolanda	35	3

Vigor	Dexterity	Mind	Charisma	Will	Alertness
1	1	2	2	1	1

Milestones

- Marry a Status 2+ man, gain +1 Status.
- Find True Love with Oswald the blacksmith (Character 21). If this happens, play a duel between Oswald (character 21) and Ward (character 35) (you can play it as Oswald or Ward, and then return to play Yolanda if you wish). Ignore this if Ward is dead.
- Collect 3 Grimoires to gain 1 random spell of any color (your choice).
- Gain 1 Charisma reroll if you win any social conflict with another notable of Status 2+.
- Give 35 Gold to the church to gain a +1 to your next 3 Will rolls.

Traits

Hidden Strength: You have 3 universal rerolls.

Amulet: Your grandmother left you an amulet that can ward off evil. Only you know about this Secret (another character may discover this by spending 3 Clues). When attacked by any supernatural creature, you may use the amulet to get 4 universal rerolls during that encounter. These rerolls are cumulative, so you can use as many as needed on any single roll (decide after rolling). Once you use the amulet, its powers are gone forever. You may also decide to give the amulet to someone else.

Contacts

Your family owns a large farmstead. You have a stable in your direct possession.

You have a passionate Secret relationship with Ward (character 35). Your official suitors include characters 21, 65 and 12.

You are a friend of Elianna (character 11) and Countess Lucretia (character 44). You dislike Ilinn the baker's daughter (character 42) considering her rude and improper.

41

Name	Gold	Status
Louise the tavern worker	30	0

Vigor	Dexterity	Mind	Charisma	Will	Alertness
2	1	2	1	2	2

Milestones

- Collect 50 Gold to gain 1 Fate.
- Collect 3 Grimoires to gain 1 random spell. The spell will be of the same color as one of the Grimoires in your possession (you choose which).
- Survive 4 combat encounters to gain +1 Vigor.
- Gain 2 Charisma rerolls if you win any social conflict with another notable of Status 1+.

Traits

Dark Secret: You are the granddaughter of Agatha the Swamp Witch. If this is discovered, you become a Suspect for the Inquisition.

Magic Talent: You have 5 rerolls that you can use without limitations in any spell casting or on any rolls performed when dealing with supernatural creatures.

Spell Knowledge: You know the Fascination and Witch's Ladder spells at the beginning of the game. You can teach them to another woman who already knows at least another spell. The teaching/learning process will take 2d6 days for both women.

Contacts

You work at lunchtime in a tavern, helping with serving and cooking, but your real income comes from selling your favors to the weary customers of the tavern in a room upstairs. You are a friend of Lizbeth the herbalist (character 46) and Isabelle (character 51). You dislikes Dididmus the astrologer (character 55) with whom you had a big disagreement on astrological matters. You are on good terms with Ozanna (character 26). Harold the retired soldier (character 52) is your suitor, but you find him too old and prefer to remain unmarried to gain some extra money from your night-time activities.

The Notables

Name	Gold	Status
Ilinn, the baker's daughter	10	1

Vigor	Dexterity	Mind	Charisma	Will	Alertness
2	2	1	1	1	2

Milestones

- Find True Love with a man with Charisma 2+ to gain 3 universal rerolls. As Ilinn is alreasy married, this relationship would be a Secret and cause Scandal if known.
- Collect 50 Gold to gain 1 Fate.
- Collect 3 Grimoires to gain 1 random spell of a color of your choice.
- Survive being wounded 3 times to gain +1 Vigor.

Traits

Beautiful Voice: You can reroll your failed Charisma rolls. Once per game, you can sing a sweet song for someone, removing the Morose condition from that character.

Stubborn: You have 5 Will rerolls.

I saw where they Hid the Book: You saw some pagans hide a book under an oak in the forest. At any moment in the game, you may visit the forest to retrieve this book. It is a grimoire (roll for its content and type as per the rules in the magic section).

Contacts

You are the daughter of Wilburn the baker (character 34). Despite your young age, you have been married to the much older Kendrick the woodcutter (character 33). You don't love him but respect him as a hard-working man.

You have an unfriendly relationship with Countess Yolanda (character 36). You are a friend of Lizbeth the herbalist (character 46) and Jehanne the butcher's daughter (character 14).

The Notables

43

Name	Gold	Status
Theobald the orphan	2	0

Vigor	Dexterity	Mind	Charisma	Will	Alertness
1	3	2	1	1	2

Milestones

- Donate 25 Gold to the Church to gain +1 Will.
- Donate 10 Gold to the poor to gain 1 Fate. You may do this only once per game.
- Collect 3 Grimoires to gain 1 random spell of a random color.
- Survive 4 combat encounters to gain +1 Vigor.
- Befriend 5 Notables to gain +1 Charisma.
- Slay one Beast (Basilisk, Tatzelwurm, Nachzehrer, Swamp Drake) to gain 1 Fate. You can do this as many times as desired.

Traits

<u>Detective</u>: Revealing Secrets costs 1 fewer Clue than normal to you. For example, to reveal a Secret with a cost of 5 Clues, you need 4 Clues. On the main investigation (to determine who is the Major Foe of the game), your 3rd Clue spent excludes 2 Foes, not one.

<u>Quick Footed</u>: You may reroll once each failed die to flee from a combat situation or to avoid capture, including Alertness and Dexterity rolls that may be required to avoid being noticed or caught by guards.

Contacts

You are on unfriendly terms with Erania the forest lady (character 62). You were raised with her in an orphanage, and you have always disliked each other.

You are a friend of Father Cyprian (character 32), Bernard the cook (character 65), Matthew the scarred boy (character 66) and Kendrick the woodcutter (character 33).

The Notables

Name	Gold	Status
Countess Lucretia	45	2

Vigor	Dexterity	Mind	Charisma	Will	Alertness
1	1	1	2	2	2

Milestones

- Find True Love with a man with minimum Charisma 2, Mind 2 and Status 2.
- Collect 50 Gold to gain +1 Will.
- Collect 100 Gold to gain 1 Fate.
- Collect 3 Grimoires to gain 1 random spell of a random color.
- Survive the first scene/event/combat encounter causing you to lose Vigor to gain +1 Vigor.

Traits

<u>Wealthy</u>: You have access to additional Gold through your possessions (houses, farmsteads, and so on). Each month, by testing Mind vs. 1, you may generate 10 Gold. If you roll a 1, however, you lose 10 Gold. If you do not have Gold to pay for this, you must repay this loss at the first opportunity or lose 1 Status. If you reach Status 0, you may no longer use this ability.

Contacts

You have a trade relationship with Lizbeth the herbalist (character 46), Aelfric the greengrocer (character 63) and Bernard the cook (character 65).

You are a friend of Crisanta (character 61). You think Crisanta helped you to keep your wealth with her magic knowledge.

You gave a job on one of your farms to Matthew the scarred boy (character 66).

The Notables

Name	Gold	Status
Gwendoline	30	2

Vigor	Dexterity	Mind	Charisma	Will	Alertness
2	2	1	1	1	2

Milestones

- Find True Love with Amari (character 23) to gain 3 universal rerolls.
- Collect 3 Grimoires to gain 1 random spell of a color of your choice.
- Survive 4 combat encounters to gain a +1 bonus to one Attribute (choose Vigor, Dexterity or Will).
- Gain 1 Fate each time you slay one of the following Dangers: Tatzelwurm, Bewitched Scarecrow, Jack Frost, Wandering Werewolf, Wanton Vampire, Nachzehrer, Minor Demon, Swamp Drake, Terror Tree.

Traits

<u>Late Husband's Sword:</u> In any combat encounter, you may reroll 2 dice.

<u>Monster Hunter:</u> During any moment of the game, you may go on a Hunt for the following creatures: Tatzelwurm, Bewitched Scarecrow, Jack Frost (only during winter months), Wandering Werewolf, Wanton Vampire, Nachzehrer, Minor Demon, Swamp Drake, Terror Tree, One-Eyed Mary. Where not otherwise indicated, you must spend 2 Clues to locate the creature before you can fight it.

Contacts

The widow of a soldier, you now work as a personal maid for Lady Elianna (character 11).

You are a friend of Erania the forest lady (character 62) and Eleanor the silk trader (character 22).

You are attracted to Amari (character 23) who sometimes trains with you.

46

Name	Gold	Status
Lizbeth, the herbalist	15	0

Vigor	Dexterity	Mind	Charisma	Will	Alertness
2	1	2	2	2	2

Milestones

- Collect 4 rare herbs to prepare 1 healing treatment that can bring back into play a dead character. This can be performed only once per game, and only as long as the character did not die more than 1 day ago. This will not look like a miracle. The character will heal by natural means.
- Collect 2 Grimoires to gain 1 Will.
- Survive 2 combat encounters to gain +1 Vigor.
- Win a debate (Charisma vs. Charisma) with Moishe the apothecary to gain 1 Charisma or Will (choose) reroll.

Traits

Healer: All characters sharing a scene with you get to reroll any die related to healing or recovering from disease or wounds, thanks to your knowledge of herbal medicine.

Herbalist: You can reroll any roll for Picking Herbs.

Suspected : You are suspected of paganism due to your practice of folk medicine.

Contacts

Venceslaus the goldsmith (Character 12) loves you but you don't love him back. If you manage to avoid sharing a scene with him (for example, not participating at a social event where he is present), you gain 1 Will reroll.

You are a friend of Didimus the astrologer (character 55), Ilinn (character 42) Jehanne the butcher's daughter (character 14), Aelfric the greengrocer (character 63) and Louise (character 41). You have a trade relationship with Erania (character 62), who occasionally finds rare herbs for you.

The Notables

51

Name	Gold	Status		
Isabelle the Bright Girl	8	1		

Vigor	Dexterity	Mind	Charisma	Will	Alertness
1	1	3	2	2	2

Milestones

- Find True Love with a man with minimum Charisma 2, Mind 2 and Status 2.
- Collect 50 Gold to gain +1 Will.
- Collect 3 Grimoires to gain 1 random spell of a color of your choice.
- Survive 3 combat encounters to gain +1 Vigor.
- Gain 2 Charisma rerolls if you win any social conflict with another notable of Status 1+.

Traits

<u>Twin Sisters</u>: At any moment in the game, you may switch places with your twin sister Viola (character 53) during any action, rolling dice in her stead. For example, if Viola risks being arrested, you may take her place. On the following day, you may switch back to Isabelle or continue playing Viola.

<u>Dark Secret</u>: Her sister Viola (character 53) has studied some witchcraft. If this is known, Isabelle will also become Suspect.

Contacts

You work as a helper in your uncle's paper mill.
You have a twin sister, Viola (character 53).
You are a friend of Ozanna (character 26) and Louise (character 41).
Matthew the scarred boy (character 66) loves you, but you don't love him back.

The Notables

Name	Gold	Status
Harold, the retired soldier	30	2

Vigor	Dexterity	Mind	Charisma	Will	Alertness
2	1	1	1	2	2

Milestones

- Marry a Status 2+ woman, gain Status +1. If the woman dies or the marriage causes Scandal, lose the bonus. You may not marry again sooner than d6 months later. If the marriage was True Love, you may not remarry during this game.
- Find True Love with a woman with minimum Charisma 1, Mind 1 and Status 1.
- Collect 50 gold to gain +1 Will.
- Collect 3 Grimoires to gain 1 random spell.
- Survive 4 combats to gain +1 Dexterity.
- Gain 2 Charisma rerolls if you win any social conflict with another notable of Status 2+.

Traits

Old Armor: You may reroll two dice in every combat encounter, or (if you didn't reroll any dice in that combat encounter), you may reroll a result on the Death Table.

I'm Not As Old As You Think: You have 4 rerolls that you may use to reroll any combat, Vigor or Dexterity die.

Contacts

You are a retired soldier who makes a living as a candlemaker.
You like Louise (character 41) who doesn't like you back.
Your only friend is Erasmus the wanderer (character 54).

53

Name			Gold		Status	
Viola, the Scarred Beauty			6		1	
Vigor	Dexterity	Mind	Charisma		Will	Alertness
1	1	1	2		2	2

Milestones

- Collect 50 Gold to gain +1 Will.
- Find True Love with Amari (character 23) to gain 1 Fate.
- Collect 2 Grimoires to gain 1 spell of your choice.
- Flee 4 combat encounters to gain +1 Dexterity.
- Flee 4 combat encounters to gain +1 Alertness.
- Gain 1 Fate if you win any social conflict with another notable of Status 2+.

Traits

<u>Witch</u>: You start the game with 2 random spells. This is a Secret and will cause you to be hunted by the inquisition if known.

<u>Twin Sisters</u>: At any moment in the game, you may switch places with your twin sister Isabelle (character 51) during a scene, rolling dice in her stead. For example, if Isabelle risks being arrested, you may reveal that it was you all along and roll dice in her place.

Contacts

You ran away from home to avoid contact with your abusive stepfather, who is responsible for the scar on your face, but remains in contact with your twin sister Isabelle (character 51).

You are in love with Amari the mercenary (character 23) but you haven't revealed your feelings yet. You are a friend of Erania the forest lady (character 62) and Aelfric the greengrocer (character 63) who loves you, even if you don't love him back.

The Notables

Name	Gold	Status
Erasmus the wanderer	2	0

Vigor	Dexterity	Mind	Charisma	Will	Alertness
1	1	1	1	2	2

Milestones

- Survive two disease infections to gain +1 Vigor
- Collect 3 Grimoires to gain +1 to Mind or Will (choose)
- Gain 1 Fate if you win any social conflict with another Notable. You may do this up to three times per game.

Traits

Ferocious dog: Once per game, you can avoid a dangerous encounter with a Violent Robber, Drunkard, Graveyard Guardian, Guards, Lunatic or a Mad Jester thanks to your dog, Storm. Every time you are involved in a combat encounter, you may have Storm fight instead of you. Storm fights as a character with Vigor 3, Dexterity 2, Alertness 4, can use 2 rerolls when fighting with any cat or wolf, and may reroll once a single result on the Death Table. If another Notable tries to assault you, that Notable must first defeat Storm.

Contacts

You are a friend of Didimus the Astrologer (character 55), Harold the retired soldier (character 52) and Theobald the orphan (character 43).

You dislike Countess Yolanda (character 36) because she sent you away rudely when you asked for a simple job on one of her farms (she didn't like your dog).

55

Name	Gold	Status		
Didimus the Astrologer	6	2		

Vigor	Dexterity	Mind	Charisma	Will	Alertness
1	1	3	2	3	2

Milestones

- Collect 3 Grimoires to gain 1 random spell.
- Survive 3 combats to gain +1 Vigor.

Traits

<u>Astrology</u>: Due to your knowledge of the stars, you can give advice and predict the future of any acting character sharing a scene with you. The character must pay you an amount of Gold equal to their Status for this service. The character gains 1 reroll that can be used ONLY in the character's next scene or encounter, or saved for a life-changing event (character's proposal to marry, wedding, or death scene).

<u>Wise</u>: You can reroll a single Mind or Alertness die in every scene or encounter.

Contacts

You are a friend of Lizbeth the herbalist (character 46), Erasmus the wanderer (character 54), Kendrick the woodcutter (character 33) and Percival Quickfingers (character 15).

You dislike Isabelle (51) because of a heated theological and philosophical discussion with her.

56

Name	Gold	Status			
Zanda, the tarot reader	10	0			

Vigor	Dexterity	Mind	Charisma	Will	Alertness
2	1	1	2	2	2

Milestones

- Find True Love with a man with minimum Charisma 2 and Mind 2.
- Collect 50 Gold to gain +1 Will.
- Collect 2 Grimoires to gain 1 random spell of a random color or 1 Fate (choose).
- Survive 4 combat encounters to gain +1 Vigor.
- Gain 2 Charisma rerolls if you win any social conflict with another notable of Status 2+.

Traits

Tarot Reading: By reading tarots for a character (who must pay you 1 Gold for this), you give that character 1 reroll that must be used in the character's next action or encounter. While you are the acting character, you may reroll the Event Track die once per month. However, you may NOT reroll an Event Track entry which mentions the Inquisition.

Suspected of Witchcraft: Due to your profession and the bias against minority groups, you are Suspected by the Inquisition.

Contacts

You have a long friendship with Ozanna (character 26). You sometimes speak with Isabelle (character 51) who often asks for a reading.

You like Aelfric the greengrocer (character 63).

The Notables

Name	Gold	Status		
Crisanta the basket weaver	6	1		

Vigor	Dexterity	Mind	Charisma	Will	Alertness
1	2	2	1	2	2

Milestones

- Find True Love with a man with minimum Mind 2 to gain 1 Fate.
- Collect 50 Gold to gain +1 Will.
- Collect 3 Grimoires to gain 1 random spell of a color of your choice.
- Survive 3 combat encounters to gain +1 Vigor.
- Gain 2 Charisma rerolls if you win any social conflict with another notable of Status 2+.

Traits

Queen of the Rats: You performed a magic ritual that put you in contact with Blackheart, the king of rats. You can ignore all damage and losses during rat infestation events. You can also send a rat, once per month, to perform an Espionage or Theft action. You may send rats to perform a single Assassination attempt once per game.

Suspect of Witchcraft: Your relationship with rats is a Secret. If this is discovered, this will create Scandal and make you a Suspect in the eyes of the inquisition.

Contacts

You make a living as a basket weaver.

You hate Vendaya (character 16), because Vendaya blames you for a wrong medical treatment which cost Vendaya's husband his life.

You are a friend of Hildegardis the philosopher (character 13). You buy bones and meat leftovers to feed your rats from Frey the butcher (character 24).

Name	Gold	Status
Erania, the forest lady	5	0

Vigor	Dexterity	Mind	Charisma	Will	Alertness
2	1	1	2	2	2

Milestones

- Find True Love with Oswald (character 21)
- Spend 25 Gold to gain +1 Status.
- Collect 3 Grimoires to gain 1 random spell.
- Survive 4 combat encounters to gain +1 Vigor.
- Slay any of the following: Wandering Werewolf, Tatzelwurm, Wanton Vampire, Nachzehrer, Bewitched Scarecrow, Blackheart the King of Rats to gain 3 universal rerolls. You may complete this Milestone once per each of these creatures, gaining 3 universal rerolls every time.

Traits

Lady of the Woods: You get 1 reroll during any encounter/event which mentions the forest or the swamp, or when picking herbs or mushrooms in the forest.

Hare's Foot Talisman: If you encounter a wolf or werewolf, you may reroll each combat dice if you want.

Bunch of Wolvesbane: You can avoid an encounter with a Wandering Werewolf with a successful test of Will roll vs. the Werewolf's Will or Vigor.

Contacts

You know Theobald (character 43) from the orphanage where you two grew up together, and hate him.

You are a good friend of Gwendoline (character 45). You have a trade relationship with Lizbeth (character 46, you find rare herbs for her).

You love Oswald the blacksmisth (character 21).

The Notables

Name	Gold	Status
Aelfric the greengrocer	18	1

Vigor	Dexterity	Mind	Charisma	Will	Alertness
2	2	1	2	1	1

Milestones

- Marry a Status 1+ woman to gain 10 Gold. If the woman dies or the marriage causes Scandal, lose 10 Gold. You may not marry again sooner than d6 months later. If the marriage was True Love, you may not remarry during this game.
- Find True Love with a woman with minimum Charisma 2.
- Collect 50 Gold to gain 1 Fate.
- Collect 3 Grimoires to gain 1 random spell of a random color.
- Survive 4 combat encounters to gain +1 Vigor.

Traits

Healthy Diet: You may reroll once every Vigor roll to resist poisoning, disease or the cold.
Family Heirlooms: You start the game with a Pair of Fancy Gloves, a Bottle of Fine Wine and a Small Jewel (that you can sell for 5 Gold if the need arises).

Contacts

You have a trade relationship with Countess Lucretia (character 44), Bernard the cook (character 65), Lizbeth the herbalist (character 46) and Vendaya (character 16).
You are a friend of Drustan the fishmonger (character 64) who has a vendor's stall next to your own.
You love Viola (character 53) but she doesn't love you back.

64

Name	Gold	Status
Drustan the fishmonger	16	2

Vigor	Dexterity	Mind	Charisma	Will	Alertness
2	2	1	2	1	1

Milestones

- Find True Love with Ilinn (character 42). If this happens, you gain 5 universal rerolls but the relationship is a Secret and causes Scandal if discovered.
- Collect 25 Gold to gain +1 Mind.
- Collect 3 Grimoires to gain 1 random spell.
- Survive 4 combat encounters to gain +1 Vigor.
- Eat 2 Delicacies and drink 1 Bottle of Fine Wine during a single day to gain 3 Charisma rerolls during that day.
- Spend 20 Gold on a party, festival, gifts or other social events to gain +1 Charisma for 30 days.

Traits

<u>Living beyond Your Means:</u> Every month, you lose 1 Gold. You may ignore this if that month you spent at least 6 Gold on any purchase.

<u>Sharp Fillet Knife:</u> You may reroll up to two dice in every combat. If any reroll result is a 1, you break your knife and you lose this trait until you spend 3 Gold to buy a new fillet knife.

Contacts

You have a trade relationship with Bernard the cook (character 65) and Frey the butcher (character 24).

You are a friend of Aelfric (character 63), Matthew the scarred boy (character 66) and Percival Quickfingers (character 15).

You loves Ilinn, the woodcutter's wife (character 42) who doesn't love you back.

The Notables

Name	Gold	Status
Bernard the cook	30	2

Vigor	Dexterity	Mind	Charisma	Will	Alertness
2	1	1	2	2	2

Milestones

- Marry a Status 2+ woman, gain Status +1. If the woman dies or the marriage causes Scandal, lose the bonus. You may not marry again sooner than d6 months later. If the marriage was True Love, you may not remarry during this game.
- Find True Love with a woman with minimum Charisma 2, Mind 2 and Status 2.
- Spend 25 Gold to gain +1 Mind.
- Collect 3 Grimoires to gain 1 random spell.
- Hunt down 3 Bears to gain +1 Vigor.

Traits

Expert Cook: You may produce one Delicacy per month, paying 2 Gold for the raw materials.
Loving the Good Life: Spend 5 Gold in any social event to gain Advantage on all Charisma rolls for 1 week.
Quick with a Knife: You may reroll one failed Combat die in every combat encounter.

Contacts

You have a trade relationship with Countess Lucretia (character 44), Drustan the fishmonger (character 64), and Wilburn the baker (character 34).

You are a friend of Aelfric (character 63) and Frey the butcher (character 24).

66

Name	Gold	Status
Matthew the Scarred Boy	*5*	*0*

Vigor	Dexterity	Mind	Charisma	Will	Alertness
1	*2*	*2*	*0*	*1*	*3*

Milestones

- Find True Love with a woman with minimum Charisma 1; gain 1 Fate if this happens. Gain 2 Fate if this is Isabelle.
- Collect 20 Gold to gain 1 Fate.
- Collect 3 Grimoires to gain 1 random spell.
- Survive 3 combat encounters to gain +1 Vigor.
- Spend 25 Gold in skin treatments to gain 1 Charisma. The treatment will require 30 days. You must pay upfront.

Traits

<u>Scarred</u>: You may not increase your Charisma above 1. You may not use any rerolls when seeking romantic companionship. However, Fate points still let you succeed on tests of Charisma.

<u>Blend into the Surroundings:</u> You may reroll any die to avoid detection (being seen, heard or noticed in a crowd).

Contacts

You work for Countess Lucretia (character 44).

You are a friend of Drustan the fishmonger (character 64) and Jehanne the butcher's daughter (character 14).

You love Isabelle (character 51) who doesn't love you back. As soon as you manage to find another love interest who loves you back, you will no longer love Isabelle.

Creating Your Own Character

If you want, instead of selecting a random Notable character, you may create your own. This character will be a traveler who has some acquaintances in Eldritchwood, and some reason to travel here. Give the character a name.

Assign 1 to 3 points to each Attribute (Vigor, Dexterity, Mind, Charisma, Will, Alertness). You have 10 points to spend, and must assign a minimum of 1 and a maximum of 3 to each Attribute. Your Status is 1. Roll 3d6 to determine how much Gold you have at the beginning of the game.

Your Milestones will be:

- Find True Love with a person with minimum Charisma 2.
- Gain 1 Status by marrying someone with at least 30 Gold and Status 1 or higher.
- Collect 25 Gold to increase 1 Attribute by 1, to a maximum of 3.
- Collect 3 Grimoires to gain 1 random spell.
- Survive 4 combat encounters to gain +1 Vigor.

Traits

<u>Foreigner:</u> Since nobody knows you in Eldritchwood, you have Advantage on any die to avoid being noticed. However, you will have Disadvantage on the first 3 Charisma rolls you perform in the game (until the locals start to know you, you will be just a foreigner to them).

<u>Well Equipped:</u> Before play starts, you may visit the general market and spend your Gold, if you wish.

Contacts

Roll d66 on the Notables list to find out who is your acquaintance in the village. You may also decide that this person is family, e.g., a cousin or nephew. You may come up with a reason why you know this person and why you are visiting the village, even if this is not essential for the game.

How to Play

You are supposed to have found some affordable lodging and a small occupation to pay for your living expenses. You may generate extra income by picking mushrooms or firewood. Play proceeds as normal. You will have to create your own contacts using the Befriend Someone action during holidays and other social events. Once you switch to a different character, you may decide that your original character leaves Eldritchwood and returns home, or (depending on what happened in the game so far) remains in the village because she/he is intrigued by the mysteries or romantically involved with someone.

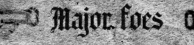

Major Foes

Name	Gold	Status
Agatha, the Swamp Witch	50	0

Vigor	Dexterity	Mind	Charisma	Will	Alertness
3	2	3	0	3	4

Abilities

Before you can fight Agatha, test Will vs. her Mind. You have Advantage if you have a Talisman, and you may reroll a failed roll if you know at least 5 spells.

If you fail, you are turned into a swamp animal and your current character exits the game. If you succeed, you can fight her using the standard combat rules.

Agatha is immune to the effects of the Hand of Glory and may not be slain by a summoned demon or by the Lightning Strike spell.

How to Encounter This Foe

To face Agatha, you must spend 3 clues to find her hut and cross the swamp.

Crossing the swamp is dangerous. You must roll 6 dice, and for every 1-2 you roll, roll d6 on the following list and face the dangers described here, rerolling duplicates:

1. The Swamp Drake (Danger 52) attacks you. The beast will flee if you wound it. If it has already been killed during the game, ignore this encounter.
2. A horde of Swamp Undead (Danger 53) walks towards you.
3. Miasmathic Air fills your lungs. Roll Vigor vs. 2 or lose either 1 Vigor or 1 Dexterity.
4. One-Eyed Mary (Danger 42) blocks your way and demands a payment: 3 Grimoires, 20 Gold, 1 Delicacy, 1 Bottle of Fine Wine. If you do not have all of these, you must fight her. If she has already been killed in the game, skip this encounter.
5. Ravens (Danger 45) and then a Bewitched Scarecrow (Danger 14) stand in your way. Play Dangers 45 and 14 one after the other.
6. The rattling of bones and teeth heralds the arrival of Terrifying Skeletons (Danger 54). They surround you, so you may not flee from this encounter. You must fight them.

2

Name	Gold	Status
The King of Thorns	30	7

Vigor	Dexterity	Mind	Charisma	Will	Alertness
4	2	2	3	3	3

Abilities

When you face the King of Thorns, you are entangled by vegetation. You cannot flee from this encounter unless you use the Witch's Flight spell.

The King is easily affected by flames. You may Sacrifice 1 Greek Fire before the combat to reduce the King's Vigor by 1.

As a supernatural creature, he is immune to the Hand of Glory and the Lightning Strike spell.

How to Encounter This Foe

To face the King of Thorns, you must reach a secret clearing in the forest near Eldritchwood, and speak the Secret Three Words. If you do not know the words, you cannot summon and fight him. Each word can be found during specific events in the game or by spending 2 Clues per word or by casting the Reveal Secret spell. You may also decide that you find a Secret Word INSTEAD of spells when you find a Grimoire.

Crossing the forest is dangerous. Roll 5 dice. For every result of 1 or 2 you roll, face one of the dangers described here, in random order (reroll duplicates):
1. The Swamp Drake (Danger 52) roars at you. The beast will fight to the death.
2. A group of Pagans (Danger 44) surround you.
3. The Tree of Terror (Danger 56) attacks you.
4. A tree falls on you! Test Dexterity vs. 1 or lose 1 Vigor.
5. A wild Boar (Danger 15) rushes out of the underbrush and attacks you.
6. A Bear (Danger 13) snarls at you and attacks.

Major Foes

3

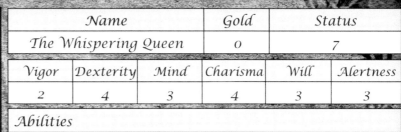

Name	Gold	Status
The Whispering Queen	0	7

Vigor	Dexterity	Mind	Charisma	Will	Alertness
2	4	3	4	3	3

Abilities

When you fight the Whispering Queen, you must test Mind vs. her Charisma. If you fail, you realize you have lost one Special Item that you had with you. Roll d6 for every Special Item, rerolling ties. The item that rolls the lowest number is lost forever. If you succeed, or if you have a Pair of fancy Gloves, you may ignore this rule.

If you have an Amulet Against the Fae, you may use it to flee from this encounter at any moment, but if you do so, your current character may NEVER meet the Whispering Queen again in the game.

She is immune to the Hand of Glory and the Lightning Strike spell.

How to Encounter This Foe

To face the Whispering Queen, you must spend 2 Clues to find a secret stone in the forest, then offer a Delicacy and a Bottle of Fine Wine to the spirits guarding it. Without these prerequisites, you will not meet her.

Crossing the forest is dangerous. Roll 6 dice. For every 1 or 2 you roll, roll d6 again and face the corresponding dangers described here (reroll duplicates):

1. A Mad Jester confronts you. Play Danger 33.
2. You hear Whispers through the forest. Play Danger 62.
3. You stumble upon a patch of Slumber Mushrooms. Roll Vigor vs. 2 or fall asleep. If you fall asleep and you rolled no other encounters, you will wake up one day later and all your Gold will be gone. If there are other encounters, your character will be lost forever.
4. A Bear rushes out of the woods to attack you. Play Danger 13.
5. A Mischievous Fairy appears to play her tricks on you. Play Danger 35.
6. Roll Dexterity vs.1 to avoid slipping on moss-covered stones. If you fail, you fall, hit your head on a sharp stone and lose 1 Vigor. Ignore the effect of the fall if you are wearing A Good Helmet.

4

Name	Gold	Status
Countess Elizabeth	30	4

Vigor	Dexterity	Mind	Charisma	Will	Alertness
4	3	2	3	3	2

Abilities

You may escape from this combat encounter only if you have a Bunch of Garlic Flowers or a Holy Relic.

To be able to inflict any damage to the Countess, you must have at least one of the following:

The Scourge of the Dead spell

A Wooden Stake

An Athame

A Holy Relic.

If you do not have any of these, you may only flee or die.

She is immune to all spells.

How to Encounter This Foe

Crossing the mountains to reach the Countess' castle is dangerous. Roll 4d6. For every 1 or 2 you roll, roll d6 on this list and face the dangers described here (reroll duplicates):

1. A Storm breaks in the sky (play Danger 51). As you seek shelter, you meet a Wanton Vampire (play Danger 63).
2. Ravens disturb you with their cawing. Play Danger 45.
3. Fear grips your heart. Test Will vs. 2. If you fail, you cannot use ANY rerolls during the confrontation with the Countess. If you succeed, play as normal.
4. You slip. Test Dexterity vs. 1. If you fail, you hurt your leg and lose the ability to flee from encounters until you pay 3 Gold to the Apothecary (25) or Herbalist (46).
5. A Brigand demands that you give him all your Gold. Lose all Gold or Play Danger 11.
6. A Nachzehrer stands in your way. Play Danger 41.

To face the Countess, you must first be admitted to her castle. To be admitted, you must send a gift worth at least 50 Gold and succeed a Charisma roll vs.2 to persuade her servants. Even if the Charisma roll fails, the gift is lost. You get a number of rerolls equal to your Status that you can use only on this Charisma roll. Alternatively, you may skulk in. You must spend 6 Clues to discover a Secret passage, or 3 if you know the Find the Path spell.

5

Name	Gold	Status
The Beast of Eldritchwood	30	?

Vigor	Dexterity	Mind	Charisma	Will	Alertness
4	3	2	3	3	2

Abilities

You may not wound the Beast unless you have a Silver Weapon or an Athame. If you face the Beast without a Silver Weapon or an Athame, ignore any wounding effect on the Beast: you may only die or flee.

The Lightning Strike spell may be used against the Beast to reduce the Beast's Vigor by 2.

How to Encounter This Foe

To face the Beast, first you must discover his/her true identity. He or she is one of the Notables. You may spend 4 Clues to reveal the monster's identity at any time. When you do so, roll d66 on the list of characters. Yes the werewolf could also be YOU! If you happen to be the werewolf, you may decide that the story ends with a savage victory for the forces of evil, or choose another character (possibly one whose friends or relatives were killed by the werewolf) and continue the hunt.

Once you know the beast's identity, you must find the Beast on the moorland. Roll 4 dice. For every 1-2 you roll, face a random danger by rolling d6 on the following list, rerolling duplicates:

1. A terrible Storm makes your trip more difficult. Play Danger 51.
2. A Brigand who sided with the werewolf confronts you. Play Danger 11.
3. A distant howling causes your heart to tremble. Test Will vs. 2. If you fail, you may not use rerolls during the final confrontation with the Beast.
4. Roll Dexterity vs. 1 to avoid falling badly and losing 1 Vigor.
5. You meet a Wandering Werewolf – play Danger 65.
6. A pack of hungry Wolves circles you. Play Danger 66. You may not flee from this encounter.

Major Foes

Name	Gold	Status
Salmac, Marquis of Hell	50	6

Vigor	Dexterity	Mind	Charisma	Will	Alertness
4	3	3	2	3	2

Abilities

Salmac is immune to all the damage that you can inflict and to all spells, unless at least one of the following applies:

You have a Holy Relic

You know the Summon Demon or Ritual Circle spells

You have an Athame

You know 5 or more spells.

When you meet Salmac, you must first Test your Will vs. his Charisma. If you fail, you will gain 50 Gold or a single Special Item of your choice, but you will find yourself at home and never again be able to encounter Salmac. If you succeed, you can fight him. The Lightning Strike spell can be used to reduce his Vigor by 2.

How to Encounter This Foe

To face this demon, you must first defeat the coven that worships him. These are 3 Notables. You must spend 2 Clues and roll d66 to discover the identity of each coven member, and you must have them Excommunicated, Jailed or Killed. If you roll the number corresponding to your own character, reroll – you can't be one of them. Upon defeating the third member of the coven, you will learn they planned to summon Salmac in a house. As you inspect the building, demonic forces will try to hinder you. Roll 5d6, and for every 1-2 rolled, roll d6 on the following list and face the corresponding danger, rerolling duplicates:

1. A Drunkard (Danger 21) bumps into you and starts a fight.
2. Pagans (Danger 44) ambush you.
3. Fear grips your heart. Lose 1 Will unless you drink a Bottle of Fine Wine. Then you meet the Master of Despair (Danger 71).
4. A Charming Assassin (Danger 16) tries to kill you.
5. A Minor Demon (Danger 34) appears and taunts you.
6. A friend betrays you. A random contact will attack you. You must fight to the death. If for any reason you have no contacts, you will be attacked by the last Notable you interacted with.

Dangers

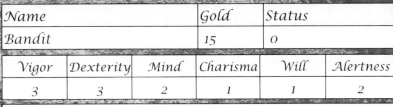

11

Name			Gold	Status	
Bandit			15	0	

Vigor	Dexterity	Mind	Charisma	Will	Alertness
3	3	2	1	1	2

Description

To hunt down a Bandit, you must test Alertness vs. his Dexterity. If you fail, he escapes. If you succeed, you can fight him. If he is Wounded, he will try to bribe his way out, offering you 10 Gold to let him live. Accept the Gold or fight him to the death. His head is worth 15 Gold.

If you meet him as a random encounter, you have to fight him. Again, he will try to bribe you for his life if wounded.

There are a total of 10 wanted men in Eldritchwood. Once all 10 have been dealt with, ignore this encounter.

12

Name			Gold	Status	
Basilisk			35	0	

Vigor	Dexterity	Mind	Charisma	Will	Alertness
1	3	0	0	1	3

Description

This creature is rare. You may hunt it only when allowed by an event. You must first locate its lair with 2 successful Mind tests vs. its Alertness. If you throw a Weasel or a bunch of Rue down its lair, you may reroll ALL your dice during the encounter. If you are Wounded by the Basilisk or if you Wound the Basilisk, you must test Vigor vs. 2 or its venom will reduce your Vigor by 1. Wounds caused by the Basilisk may be healed only with the help of the Apothecary (5 Gold per Wound).
The head of a Basilisk is worth a reward of 35 Gold.

Dangers

13

Name	Gold	Status
Bear	6	0

Vigor	Dexterity	Mind	Charisma	Will	Alertness
4	3	0	0	1	2

Description

To hunt down a bear, you must roll 3 successful contests of Dexterity vs. the bear's Alertness, and then fight with it to the death.

If you are attacked by a bear, you have two options: 1)fight, or 2) negate the encounter by sacrificing a Jar of Honey (the bear will eat the honey and leave you alone). If you have a Jar of Honey and Slumber Mushroom Powder, you can slay the beast without having to fight it (the bear will eat the honey laced with the poison and fall into a deep slumber).

The skin of a bear may be sold for 6 Gold in town.

14

Name	Gold	Status
Bewitched Scarecrow	0	0

Vigor	Dexterity	Mind	Charisma	Will	Alertness
4	2	0	0	0	0

Description

This is a scarecrow that has been animated by dark magic. It looks like an ordinary scarecrow until you are too close to escape.

You can sacrifice 1 Greek Fire to automatically destroy the Scarecrow.

If you have a Jack-O'-Lantern, you may ignore this encounter.

Dangers

15

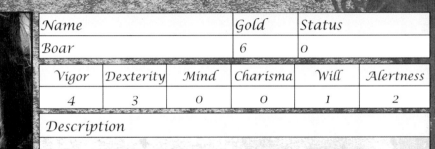

Name	Gold	Status
Boar	6	0

Vigor	Dexterity	Mind	Charisma	Will	Alertness
4	3	0	0	1	2

Description

To hunt down a boar, you must test Dexterity twice vs. the boar's Alertness. If you succeed, you can fight the boar to the death (once the combat encounter begins, you may not escape, unless you use Witch's Flight).

If you are attacked by a boar, you may fight it to the death or avoid the encounter by sacrificing 1 Delicacy (boars are always hungry for a tasty morsel).

You may sell a slain boar for its meat for 6 Gold.

16

Name	Gold	Status
Charming Assassin	30	0

Vigor	Dexterity	Mind	Charisma	Will	Alertness
1	3	2	3	1	3

Description

Test your Will vs. her Charisma. If you fail, increase her Vigor and Dexterity by 1 until the end of the encounter.

You may bribe the Assassin by giving her 1 Silver Dagger or 50 Gold, or any other item worth 50 Gold or more. If you bribe her, you may also hire her for an Assassination attempt (this requires a successful Charisma test vs. her Mind. If the roll fails, she does not accept the job).

She has a leather pouch containing 30 Gold.

21

Name	Gold	Status
Drunkard	0	1

Vigor	Dexterity	Mind	Charisma	Will	Alertness
2	1	0	1	0 to 2	0

Description

The roads of Eldritchwood are full of men and women who try to drown the ills of life with ale, wine and other spirits. Some want to pick a fight.

If you defeat the Drunkard, you gain a Bottle of Fine Wine. Note that the Drunkard's Will score is random, due to the effects of alcohol. If you need to determine his Will score, roll d6, counting 1-2 as 0, 3-5 as 1, and 6 as 2.

Sacrifice a Bottle of Fine Wine to avoid this encounter.

22

Name	Gold	Status
Enigmatic Wanderer	10	1

Vigor	Dexterity	Mind	Charisma	Will	Alertness
1	1	1	1	1	1

Description

You meet a mysterious traveler who has something for you. Roll d6 to determine what it is. 1) He offers you 10 Gold to hunt down a wolf that has been killing his sheep; 2) He offers to sell you a Grimoire for 10 Gold; 3) He gifts you an Amulet (gain 1 reroll); 4) He delivers you a mysterious letter full of surprising information (gain 1 Clue); 5) He has a business proposal (give him now 10 Gold and get from him 15 Gold after 1d6 days; 6) He asks you for help (fight against a Drunkard or a Bandit, your choice, and he will reward you with 10 Gold). After the event, he disappears.

Dangers

23

Name			Gold	Status	
Guards			1	1	

Vigor	Dexterity	Mind	Charisma	Will	Alertness
2	2	1	1	1	1

Description

If the guards try to catch you, you may surrender (and will be Jailed), try to flee (test Dexterity vs. their Dexterity to escape), try to Bribe them (test Charisma vs. their Will, and if successful spend 5 Gold) or fight them.

Guards ignore the first Wound you inflict on them, thanks to their armor.

If you are defeated by Guards, you do not die (do not roll on the Death Table), but you are Jailed.

If you defeat the Guards, you are free, but you are now Wanted.

24

Name			Gold	Status	
Graveyard Guardian			1	1	

Vigor	Dexterity	Mind	Charisma	Will	Alertness
1	1	2	2	2	3

Description

When you meet the Graveyard Guardian, test your Will roll vs. his Charisma 2. If you succeed, nothing happens. If you fail, you are intimidated and at a Disadvantage on any roll during this encounter and during any Scene set at the graveyard.

If you are caught doing any illegal action in the graveyard, you may Bribe him with a successful test of Charisma vs. his Will 2 and 5 Gold, or fight him. If you kill him, another Guardian will be appointed after 2d6 days. Before the new Guardian is appointed, ignore all encounters with the Graveyard Guardian.

25

Name			Gold	Status	
Jack Frost			0	0	

Vigor	Dexterity	Mind	Charisma	Will	Alertness
3	1	2	2	1	1

Description

Upon appearing, Jack Frost will throw a number of snowballs at you equal to your current Vigor. Test Dexterity vs. his Dexterity to avoid each snowball. Lose 1 temporary Vigor per each snowball that hits you. If this brings your Vigor to 0, you do not die, but are knocked out cold. When you wake up, you regain 1 Vigor, but all your Special Items will be missing and Jack Frost will be gone. He will not steal your Gold. As soon as you drink any alcohol or spend 1 Gold in the tavern, you recover all the Vigor lost to the snowballs.

You may fight Jack Frost, if you want, only after he has thrown his snowballs at you.

26

Name			Gold	Status	
Jack O'Lantern Spirit			0	0	

Vigor	Dexterity	Mind	Charisma	Will	Alertness
1	0	0	0	1	1

Description

A drunk blacksmith who tried to cheat the devil wanders the Earth as a restless spirit. He uses a carved turnip or pumpkin as a lantern. Fight the Jack O'Lantern. If you do not destroy it on the first combat turn, it will summon someone to fight in its stead. Roll d6: 1-2 Ravens, 3-4 Swamp Undead, 5 Bewitched Scarecrow, 6 Jack Frost (only in winter, or a Bewitched Scarecrow during other seasons). If you defeat the summoned creature, you may take the Jack O'Lantern and carry it with you as a Special Item.

Sacrifice a Bottle of Fine Wine or a Horseshoe to avoid this encounter.

31

Name			Gold	Status	
Lunarist			2	0	

Vigor	Dexterity	Mind	Charisma	Will	Alertness
1	0	2	1	1	1

Description

The lunarist is an old, cross-eyed man who gives advice about everything, from beauty treatments to gardening, based on the lunar calendars he compiles. You may spend 1 Gold to ask him some advice. This will give you a single universal reroll. You must use this reroll in the next 10 days. If you do not use it, it's lost.

32

Name			Gold	Status	
Lunatic			0	0	

Vigor	Dexterity	Mind	Charisma	Will	Alertness
3	1	0	0	2	1

Description

As you walk through the village, a raving figure jumps out of the shadows and assaults you. The madman possesses an unnatural strength fueled by demonic possession. You can fight him or try to calm him down with a successful Charisma test vs. his Will, rolled with Disadvantage. If you try to calm him down and fail, you will have to reroll your highest rolling die in the ensuing fight.

You may avoid this encounter by giving him a Bottle of Fine Wine, a Delicacy, or a Fancy Hat.

Dangers

33

Name		Gold	Status
Mad Jester		0	0

Vigor	Dexterity	Mind	Charisma	Will	Alertness
1	3	1	2	3	1

Description

Perform a combat encounter with the Jester, but you must fight using your Will vs. his Charisma. If you are Wounded, you lose 1 Will instead. If your Will reaches 0, you become another Jester and attack one of your Contacts – that character becomes Active and must play this encounter again, against your previous character who now is a Jester. Repeat this process until needed. If you defeat the Jester, he runs away and you may keep his Fancy Hat.

34

Name		Gold	Status
Minor Demon		30	n/a

Vigor	Dexterity	Mind	Charisma	Will	Alertness
4	3	3	2	3	3

Description

When you encounter a Minor Demon, roll d6. On a 1-3, it appears in human form and tempts you (test Will vs. the demon's Charisma or lose 1 Will). On a 4-6, it appears in demonic form (test Will vs. the demon's Will or lose the ability to use rerolls during the encounter due to fear). In both cases, you must then fight him physically. Sacrifice a Holy Relic to avoid this encounter. Sacrifice Holy Water to automatically reduce its Vigor to 1.

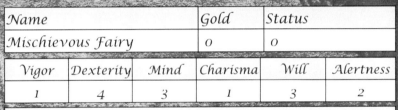

Dangers

35

Name	Gold	Status
Mischievous Fairy	0	0

Vigor	Dexterity	Mind	Charisma	Will	Alertness
1	4	3	1	3	2

Description

If you have a Pair of Fancy Gloves, you can avoid this encounter by rolling Mind vs. the Fairy's Mind. If you have an Iron Horseshoe, you can avoid this encounter with a Will roll vs. the Fairy's Will. If you play this encounter, roll d6 to determine what will happen: 1) She plays music, making you dance to exhaustion, test Vigor vs. her Charisma or lose 1 Vigor until you spend 3 days resting; 2-3) She curses you and your face becomes green (lose 1 point of Charisma); 3-4) She traps you in a dreamworld, you emerge 1d6 days later and you lose 1 point of Mind; 5-6) She guides you to a pot of Gold (gain 25 Gold if you kill the Boar guarding it, Danger 15).

36

Name	Gold	Status
Moneylender	50	1

Vigor	Dexterity	Mind	Charisma	Will	Alertness
1	1	3	1	3	1

Description

If you need money, fast, he is the man for you. You can borrow up to 50 Gold. You must pay back the amount of Gold you took, with a 10% surcharge (round up), after 10 days. If you do not pay, the surcharge becomes 50% and you have another 10 days. If after that you still do not pay, you will have an encounter with a Violent Robber and, if that does not kill you, with a Charming Assassin.

If you kill the Moneylender, you can steal his treasure (50 Gold), but you immediately become Wanted.

41

Name			Gold	Status	
Nachzehrer			0	0	

Vigor	Dexterity	Mind	Charisma	Will	Alertness
3	2	1	1	1	1

Description

This vampire sucks the lifeforce out of people passing by his grave. When he has enough energy, he is free to wander around in search of victims. Test Vigor vs. 1. On a success, nothing happens. On a failure, the Nachzehrer jumps out of his grave and you must fight him. You will have a -1 to Vigor or Dexterity (your choice).

The Nachzehrer spreads disease. If you encounter him, test Vigor vs. 1. On a failure, you contract a wasting disease that will kill you in 2d6 days unless you spend 10 Gold for a treatment by an herbalist or apothecary. If you slay him, you may take his shroud as a Special Item. It gives you a Vigor reroll vs. any disease you may contract in the future.

42

Name			Gold	Status	
One-Eyed Mary			15	0	

Vigor	Dexterity	Mind	Charisma	Will	Alertness
3	1	1	0	1	2

Description

An old witch turned into a monster, One-Eyed Mary can be Bribed by giving her a Grimoire or an Amulet. If you do so, she will leave you alone. If you do not do so, she will curse you. Test Will vs. her Will. If you succeed, she will leave. If you fail, you will have Disadvantage on all your dice rolls until you attend church next Sunday or until you read all the spells contained in a Grimoire.

If you slay her, you will find 15 Gold or a Silver Dagger (choose) hidden in a tree hollow. If you kill her, ignore encounters with her in the future.

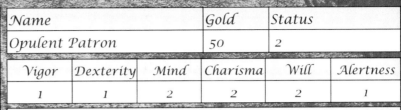

43

Name			Gold	Status	
Opulent Patron			50	2	

Vigor	Dexterity	Mind	Charisma	Will	Alertness
1	1	2	2	2	1

Description

If you have at least 2 Clues collected for any investigation in the game, this rich man is interested in helping your cause. You lose the Clues, but gain 10 Gold per every Clue lost. From now on, if you are Jailed, you can play the Opulent Patron as a character to get the Jailed character out of trouble.

If you attack the Opulent Patron, you will have to fight with Guards instead (Danger 23), but they will not try to catch you alive – they will kill you if they defeat you. Once you have slain the Guards, you may take the Opulent Patron's Gold. If you meet him again after this, treat it as an encounter with Guards (Danger 23).

44

Name			Gold	Status	
Pagans			15	0	

Vigor	Dexterity	Mind	Charisma	Will	Alertness
4	3	3	1	3	2

Description

Pagans surround you with evil intent. They plan to sacrifice you to the demon they serve! If this happens, advance the Event Track by 2d6. You may not flee from this encounter.

If you have a Holy Relic, you may sacrifice it to reroll all the dice rolls in this encounter.

If you defeat the Pagans, you gain 1 Clue and find 15 Gold and 1 Silver Dagger among their possessions.

Dangers

45

Name			Gold	Status
Ravens			0	N/a

Vigor	Dexterity	Mind	Charisma	Will	Alertness
1	3	0	0	1	2

Description

Ravens start circling around you and cawing. This is a sign of ill omen. Lose all your rerolls, except those that are connected with equipment (like combat rerolls from weapons or armor).

If you have an Amulet, you may sacrifice it to avoid this encounter.

46

Name			Gold	Status
Slumber Mushrooms			1d6	N/a

Vigor	Dexterity	Mind	Charisma	Will	Alertness
0	0	0	0	0	0

Description

These orange mushrooms release their poisonous spores in the air. Test Vigor vs. 2 or fall asleep. If you fall asleep and you rolled no other encounters, you wake up one day later: all your Gold will be gone. Your Special Items remain with you.

You may pick up a few Slumber Mushrooms and resell them to the herbalist (character 46) or the apothecary (character 25) for 1d6 Gold.

Dangers

51

Name	Gold	Status
Storm	0	n/a

Vigor	Dexterity	Mind	Charisma	Will	Alertness
1	0	0	0	0	0

Description

A strong Storm breaks over the village. Thunder and lightning fill your heart with fear, and soon you are soaking wet. Test Vigor vs. 1 or get ill, losing the ability to use any form of rerolls for the next d6 days. Test Will vs. 0. On a success, nothing happens. On a failure, you will be at -1 to Will during your next encounter with any supernatural creature.

If you have a Good Cape, ignore both effects of the Storm.

52

Name	Gold	Status
Swamp Drake	35	n/a

Vigor	Dexterity	Mind	Charisma	Will	Alertness
4	1	0	0	1	2

Description

This ungodly beast came on a ship from a foreign land, and it grew in the swamp near Eldritchwood where the miasmatic exhalations made it even stronger. Sacrifice a Goat or Lamb to the beast to avoid this encounter. If you don't have any, you must fight or run. Every time you wound the Swamp Drake, roll d6. On a roll of 1-3 you wound it normally. On a roll of 4-6, the wound is negated by the creature's scales. Ignore this rule if you have read a Bestiary.

There is only ONE Swamp Drake. If it is slain and then you roll it again, ignore the encounter. Gain a 30 Gold reward and +1 to Status for slaying this beast.

Dangers

53

Name				Gold	Status
Swamp Undead				0	n/a

Vigor	Dexterity	Mind	Charisma	Will	Alertness
2	0	0	0	4	0

Description

Agatha the Swamp Witch uses her diabolical powers to resurrect many men who, in the years, have been claimed by the miasmas of the great swamp. This unholy reviving of the body turns the cadavers into a pathetic imitation of life. The risen dead hunger for human flesh and protect Agatha's hut. Luckily, they are slow, so you get Advantage on any attempt to flee the encounter.

You may avoid this encounter by sacrificing 1 Greek Fire.

54

Name				Gold	Status
Terrifying Skeletons				30	n/a

Vigor	Dexterity	Mind	Charisma	Will	Alertness
1	2	0	0	1	1

Description

These skeletons were created by Agatha, the Swamp Witch, using the bodies of men who perished in the swamp. They take their power from your fear. At the beginning of the encounter, test your Will three times vs.1. The Skeletons gain +1 Vigor for every failure rolled.

If you have a Heavy Mace, you can easily smash their rotten bones. You may reroll 2 dice in this combat encounter.

If you destroy the Skeletons, the authorities will reward you with 30 Gold.

55

Name			Gold	Status	
Tatzelwurm			25	N/a	

Vigor	Dexterity	Mind	Charisma	Will	Alertness
3	2	1	0	1	2

Description

To hunt down the elusive Tatzelwurm, roll 3 successful tests of Alertness vs. its Dexterity. If you fail one or more tests, you can't catch it. If you succeed, you must fight it to the death. If you roll any 1 on any attempt, you breathe the Tatzelwurm's breath and must test Vigor vs. 1 or die immediately.

You may negate the encounter by sacrificing a Holy Relic.

The body of the Tatzelwurm is worth 25 Gold if brought to the authorities.

56

Name			Gold	Status	
Tree of Terror			15	0	

Vigor	Dexterity	Mind	Charisma	Will	Alertness
4	3	3	1	3	2

Description

This horrible creature was once the tree under which the Whispering Queen and the King of Thorns renewed their marriage vows every year. When they broke up, it turned into a twisted monster that kills whoever ventures in the forest.

There is only a single Tree of Terror in the game. If it is slain and then you roll it again, ignore this encounter.

Sacrifice 1 Greek Fire to reduce its Vigor by 2.

Gain 15 Gold if you bring this creature's head to the authorities.

61

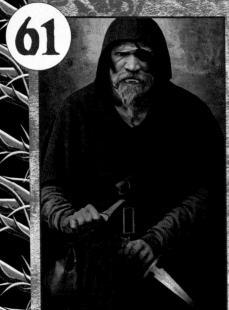

Name	Gold	Status
Violent Robber	5	0

Vigor	Dexterity	Mind	Charisma	Will	Alertness
2	3	1	1	1	2

Description

Test Alertness vs. the Robber's Dexterity. If you fail, choose: 1) Lose one special item carried (you choose which) or 2) Lose half of your Gold, rounded up. If you succeed, you can fight or try to escape. If the Violent Robber is Wounded, he will flee.

He is a wanted man. If you defeat him, you may cash in a reward of 5 Gold.

You may automatically avoid this encounter if you have no Gold or Special items.

62

Name	Gold	Status
Whispers in the Forest	0	0

Vigor	Dexterity	Mind	Charisma	Will	Alertness
0	0	0	1	1	0

Description

As you walk near the forest, a soft voice beckons from the trees. Test Will with Disadvantage vs. Charisma 1. If you succeed, nothing happens. If you fail, you get lost in the woods. Test Mind or Alertness vs. 2 to find your way home. Roll as many times as needed until you succeed, but for every failure you will have an encounter with (roll d6):

1) Mischievous Fairy; 2) Bandit; 3) Boar; 4) Bear; 5) Ravens; 6) Pagans.

Dangers

63

Name	Gold	Status
Wanton Vampire	15	1

Vigor	Dexterity	Mind	Charisma	Will	Alertness
2	2	1	2	1	3

Description

Test your Will vs. the Vampire's Charisma. If you fail, she will bite your neck and sap your lifeforce (you lose 1 Vigor and she gains 1 Vigor before the combat starts). If you succeed, you may sacrifice 1 Holy Relic to have the Vampire flee, or sacrifice 1 Holy Water to automatically reduce her Vigor by 1.

64

Name	Gold	Status
Witch Hunter	20	1

Vigor	Dexterity	Mind	Charisma	Will	Alertness
3	2	1	1	3	3

Description

If you know no spells, and possess no Grimoires or amulets, you may ignore this encounter. Any attempt to Befriend the Witch-hunter is rolled with Disadvantage (he's a gruff guy). Once he has entered play, he will also be present at any social events.

If you know spells or possess any Amulet or Grimoire, roll Charisma vs. the Witch-hunter's Alertness. If you succeed, he leaves you alone. If you fail, or if you are already Suspected of Witchcraft, you must escape or fight him. If he defeats you, roll d6. On a 1-3 you are Jailed, on a 4-6 you die.

Dangers

65

Name				Gold	Status
Wandering Werewolf				30	0

Vigor	Dexterity	Mind	Charisma	Will	Alertness
3	2	1	0	1	3

Description

Test Alertness vs. his Dexterity. If you succeed, play the encounter as normal. If you fail, he ambushes you and you must reroll with Disadvantage your highest rolling combat die.

If you have a Silver Dagger, gain 3 rerolls that may be used only during this encounter.

If you slay him, gain a reward of 30 Gold from the authorities.

66

Name				Gold	Status
Wolf				2	n/a

Vigor	Dexterity	Mind	Charisma	Will	Alertness
1	2	1	0	0	3

Description

The Wolf is hungry and it won't attack you if you throw some food at it. You may sacrifice one Lamb or Hare or a Delicacy to avoid this encounter.

Wolves fear fire. You may sacrifice one Greek Fire to scare away the wolf.

If you slay the wolf, its skin may be sold for 2 Gold.

67

Name		Gold	Status	
Blackheart, King of Rats		0	n/a	

Vigor	Dexterity	Mind	Charisma	Will	Alertness
1	4	2	1	2	4

Description

A smart, talking rat that appears to witches, Blackheart may be slain only by burning 3 Grimoires and using a Silver Dagger to fight it. If it is slain, ignore all events that have to do with rats or Danger 77 during the game, including further encounters with Blackheart. If Blackheart Wounds you, test Vigor vs. 2. On a success, nothing happens. On a failure, you develop an infection that will kill you in exactly 14 days unless you spend 30 Gold for a treatment from an apothecary or herbalist, or use the Healing spell.

Sacrifice a Splendid Housecat to reroll all dice in a combat encounter with Blackheart.

68

Name		Gold	Status	
The Dust		0	0	

Vigor	Dexterity	Mind	Charisma	Will	Alertness
1	1	3	2	4	2

Description

Some travelers recount stories of this mysterious person, who could be a man or a woman, with skin covered in dust and cracked like an old pot. Some say s/he is a demon, others say s/he is a damned soul, roaming the earth forever. If you encounter the Dust, the creature will blow dust in your face. Test Dexterity vs. the creature's Dexterity to avoid the dust. If you fail, you will die after 2d6+Vigor days unless you donate at least 50 Gold to church or use the Healing spell. If you succeed, you avoid the small cloud of dust and the creature disappears.

Dangers

69

Name			Gold	Status	
The Krampus			0	n/a	

Vigor	Dexterity	Mind	Charisma	Will	Alertness
3	3	2	0	2	2

Description

The Krampus appears only around Christmas. If you possess any Grimoires or know any spells, or have killed someone during the game (not counting beasts and witches), then he will punish you. Roll d6. On a 1-2, the Krampus grabs you and takes you for a ride in the sky, test Will vs. 2 or lose 1 Mind. On a 3-4, he leaves you on a treetop (test Dexterity vs. 1 to climb down, on a failure lose 1 Vigor or Dexterity); On a 5-6, he hits you with a broom (test Vigor vs. 1 or be forced in bed for 1d6 days as your scratches heal). If you are innocent, he will give you a bunch of Rue and disappear.

70

Name			Gold	Status	
The Wandering Witch			2d6	0	

Vigor	Dexterity	Mind	Charisma	Will	Alertness
1	1	3	2	2	2

Description

You meet a beautiful lady who practices magic. Test Charisma vs. her Will of 2. If you succeed, she will help you (choose one: heal 1 Wound, remove one Condition, receive 1 Iron Amulet Against Fairies, receive 1 random Grimoire, receive 1 bunch of Rue, learn 1 Secret Word).

If you fail, or if you want to fight her, fight. If you defeat her, you find 1 Grimoire, 2d6 Gold, 1 bunch of Rue and 1 Fine Knife among her possessions.

Dangers

71

Name	Gold	Status
The Master of Despair	0	n/a

Vigor	Dexterity	Mind	Charisma	Will	Alertness
2	1	2	2	2	2

Description

When you meet the Master of despair, Test your Will twice vs. his Charisma. For each failure, reduce an Attribute of your choice by 1, to a minimum of 0. You cannot reduce an Attribute below 0. During the month of May, if you have a bunch of Roses you may sacrifice it to reroll all Will rolls performed during this encounter.

You may fight the Master of Despair, but if you kill him he will just disappear. He will never truly die: you may meet him again in the game.

Sacrifice an Amulet to avoid this encounter.

72

Name	Gold	Status
The Great Goat of the Woods	0	n/a

Vigor	Dexterity	Mind	Charisma	Will	Alertness
3	3	2	0	3	3

Description

If you are a witch, the Great Goat will give you 1 Grimoire with 2 Black Magic spells. If no, you must appease the Great Goat with a successful Charisma roll vs. its Will or by offering a Delicacy and a Bottle of Fine Wine. If you fail to appease the Great Goat, you must either fight it or lower one of your Attributes by 1 to a minimum of 0 (you can't lower an Attribute that is at 0 already).

If you defeat him, you will find 1 item of your choice from the General Market or Black Market lists.

Dangers

73

Name	Gold	Status
The Guardian of Wheat	0	n/a

Vigor	Dexterity	Mind	Charisma	Will	Alertness
2	3	0	0	0	1

Description

This bewitched scarecrow is armed with an enchanted sword, and moves with uncanny speed.

Sacrifice 1 Greek Fire to destroy the Guardian of Wheat. If you do so, test Dexterity vs. 1 or lose 1 Vigor to the flames.

If you defeat the Guardian of Wheat, you can take its enchanted sword as a Special Item. While using the sword, you may perform 2 rerolls in every combat. In addition, this weapon counts as a Silver Dagger.

74

Name	Gold	Status
The Greedy Witch	25	0

Vigor	Dexterity	Mind	Charisma	Will	Alertness
1	1	2	0	0	1

Description

The witch is willing to sell information and magical knowledge. Pay 20 Gold to buy a Grimoire with 2 random Black or Red spells; pay 10 Gold to know one of the Three Sacred Words (you may buy multiple Words if you have enough Gold); pay 5 Gold to learn 1 Clue; pay 3 Gold for a bunch of Rue. If you do not have Gold, or do not want to pay, the witch will try to ensorcel you. Test Will vs. her Charisma. If you fail, you fall asleep and she takes all your Gold. If you succeed, you may fight her or flee. If you defeat her, you find 25 Gold and a Grimoire with 3 random spells.

75

Name	Gold	Status
The White Stag	0	n/a

Vigor	Dexterity	Mind	Charisma	Will	Alertness
3	3	2	2	3	3

Description

The White Stag taunts you. Can you catch it? Test Alertness vs. its Dexterity, and then Vigor vs. its Vigor to keep up with its fast pace through the woods. You may use any rerolls that apply to hunting. If one roll fails, the chase is fruitless and the encounter ends. If both rolls succeed, choose one of the following rewards: 1) A Condition is removed from you or any other character in play; 2) One of your Attributes increases by 1; 3) You find any one Special Item; 4) You set back the Event Track by 2d6; 5) You find a pot containing 30 Gold.

76

Name	Gold	Status
Woman of Ill Repute	12	0

Vigor	Dexterity	Mind	Charisma	Will	Alertness
1	1	1	3	1	2

Description

The Woman of Ill Repute is willing to sell a Secret. If you successfully test Charisma vs. her Mind, she will reveal the Secret of a single Notable you have interacted with, for 10 Gold. If your roll fails, she will mislead you (lose 1d6 Gold for some worthless information). You may ignore her if you do not have at least 6 Gold.

Once you know a Secret, you may use it to Blackmail someone (gaining 3 rerolls in any Social combat with that person) or make it go public.

Dangers

77

Name			Gold	Status	
Rats			0	n/a	

Vigor	Dexterity	Mind	Charisma	Will	Alertness
1	1	0	0	0	1

Description

You may ignore this encounter if you sacrifice a Delicacy.

If you sacrifice 1 dose of Poison or 1 Mandrake and 1 Delicacy, you may ignore this and the next encounter with rats.

If you have a Splendid Housecat, you may reroll all dice in the encounter.

If you have a Loyal Dog, you get a +1 to your Vigor during the encounter. This may **NOT** be cumulated with the bonus from a Splendid Housecat, use one or the other.

78

Name			Gold	Status	
Barrow Cat			Varies	n/a	

Vigor	Dexterity	Mind	Charisma	Will	Alertness
2	2	1	0	1	3

Description

The Barrow Cat is an undead wildcat watching over the grave of a witch. If you defeat it, you will find a Grimoire and a Silver Dagger. If you know the Find Hidden Thing spell, you also find 25 Gold, a jar of Honey and a Bottle of Fine Wine.

If you have a Loyal Dog, you may reroll 1 die in this encounter, but if the reroll is a 1, the Dog dies.

79

Name			Gold	Status	
Mandrake			25	0	

Vigor	Dexterity	Mind	Charisma	Will	Alertness
0	0	0	0	1	1

Description

To find a mandrake, perform 2 successful Mind rolls vs. the plant's Alertness during the Search for Herbs action. If 1 or 2 rolls fail, you can't find it. Then you need a Sharp Knife to draw 3 circles around the plant. You need to Sacrifice a Dog: you tie the plant to the dog's tail, then call the dog to you. The Dog pulls the plant of the ground, the mandrake screams and its scream kills the dog. If you do not sacrifice a Dog, you must test Vigor vs.1 or be killed by the mandrake's scream. The plant may be sold for 25 Gold or used to create 1 dose of Poison or to cast the Alraune white spell.

80

Name			Gold	Status	
Melusine			0	0	

Vigor	Dexterity	Mind	Charisma	Will	Alertness
2	2	3	3	2	1

Description

This mermaid will marry any unmarried male who succeeds in a Charisma test vs. her Will. She will appear as a beautiful human girl, not a mermaid, but once per week, on Fridays, she must bathe in a barrel or a small pond to keep her powers. Her nature is a Secret. Melusine's husband gets 3 universal rerolls per month. However, every Friday, you must test Will vs.1 to resist the urge to spy on her. On a failure, test Dexterity vs. her Alertness. If you fail, she understands you have seen her and will leave you forever. You will be Morose for 2d6 days and will never be able to Find True Love or marry again.

How to Play

Determine a start date by rolling d6:
1) Carnival (March 1st, winter)
2) Christmas (December 25, winter)
3) Easter (use the day shown on your planner)
4) Lammas Day (August 1st, summer)
5) Halloween (October 31st, autumn)
6) Saint Valentine's Day (February 14th, winter).

The game starts d6 days before the date shown.

Select a character by rolling d66 on the Notables list.

Roll d6 on the Events Track. Play the corresponding event from the Event list (for example, if you roll a 4, read event 4).

Every day, roll d6. On a roll of 1, 2 or 3 an Event happens. Roll d3, add to the current event track (the number where you are at) and play the corresponding entry from the list.

Some events apply to all the village, some affect a random Notable (roll d66 to determine whom - reroll if that person is dead or otherwise unavailable), others apply only to the Acting character.

Roll for the event BEFORE planning your character's Action for the day. This lets you react to the event. **Some Events may lead to a Scene.** A Scene is a small event. Refer to the appropriate number in the Scenes list, and then go back to the Events Track.

Fixed Events, such as holidays and other social events, happen on their date on the **calendar**. For example, on May 20th Eldritchwood celebrates the Festival of Roses, a big social event where lovers exchange promises and gifts. It is possible that an event from the event list happens on the day of a fixed Event. Just play two events during that day, in the order that seems logical to you.

Many events say that you MAY do something. When the word MAY is used, you can decide to play that event or not, as you see fit. If an event says that you MUST do something or you have to CHOOSE between multiple options, you must play through the event.

Advance through your character's actions day by day,

performing one Action per day (some Actions will require more than one day). Take notes on your planner, to keep a record of what you do, and annotate any result (such as money gained) on your play sheet, or on a piece of scrap paper. If you perform any investigations, you may have multiple investigations going on at the same time.

For example you could be investigating to discover the Main Foe behind the supernatural attacks AND trying to find out who stole the butcher's meat from his shop. The two leads may be connected or not. You will discover it only by playing!

Keep repeating this procedure until you destroy the Main Foe or reach Event 100. At that point, the game ends.

Important Calendar Dates

Mark these important dates on your planner and come back here for the rules when needed.

February 14th, St. Valentine's day. If you are in a relationship or courting someone, you MUST spend 3 times your Status in Gold to buy something for your partner. You may meet that character and switch to it as you deliver the present. If your partner's Status is higher than yours, use their Status to calculate the cost of the present. All characters in a love relationship get 1 universal reroll on this date.

March 1st, Carnival. Social event. During the revelries, you may wear a mask. You get 2 rerolls that may be used to avoid detection, to escape from any event involving guards or the inquisition, and to perform theft and assassination. If you encounter Dangers 21, 32 or 33, you may not use any rerolls in the encounter.

May 20th, the Festival of Roses. Social event. During this day, you get 3 rerolls you can use when confronting pagans, witches, undead creatures or demons. You may buy a Bunch of Roses for 1 Gold.

Lent (date varies, 6 weeks before Easter). You may not buy Delicacies or bottles of Fine Wine and no wedding may be celebrated during this period.

Easter (date varies, use the date shown in your

planner). Social Event, you may interact with any character who is not Jewish, a witch, or jailed. You may participate in a easter egg hunt. Test your Mind vs. 2 three times. If you roll 3 successes, you win. The character gains d6 Gold and 1 universal reroll. During Easter, no spells may be cast or studied. During Easter, the cost of lambs is reduced by 1 Gold.

Hocktide (date varies, the second Monday and Tuesday after Easter). Social event, you may start to court someone. If you donate to the Church an amount of Gold equal to your beloved's Status times two, you get a free reroll on a Charisma roll to seduce your beloved.

Rogationtide (three-day celebration taking place six weeks after Easter), each day is a Social Event. A procession is led by a straw-stuffed dragon representing the Devil. On the third day, straw is removed from the dragon's tail so that it goes limp. The dragon is relegated to the back of the procession. During the 3rd day, you get 1 universal reroll against any supernatural creature, and spells may not be cast. Weddings are not allowed during Rogationtide.

Pentecost (date varies, 7 days after Rogationtide). You must give to the Church an amount of Gold equal to your Status, unless you are homeless or a Jewish person. On Pentecost day you must attend Church (treat as a social event).

August 1st, Lammas Day. Social Event. If today you must roll for a random Danger, meet Danger 73 instead. Character 34 receives 2d6 Gold and 1 universal reroll on this day.

September 29th, Michaelmas Day. Feast of Saint Michael the Archangel. Social event. No spells may be cast on this day, and all demons encountered have -1 to their Vigor and Dexterity.

October 31st, Halloween. Social event. During this day, you get +1 to your Mind, Will or Charisma for any Test related to spells or interaction with supernatural creatures, including Will and Charisma tests. If you have to select a random Danger on this date, roll d6 on this table instead:

1) Play Danger 44

2) Roll d6, 1-3 play Danger 26, 4-6 play Danger 42.

3) Roll d6, 1-3 play Danger 68, 4-6 play Danger 80.

4) Roll d6, 1-3 play Danger 70, 4-6 play Danger 78.

5) Roll d6, 1-3 play Danger 34, 4-6 play Danger 71.

6) Roll d6, 1-4, play Danger 72, 5-6, play Danger 74.

December 25th, Christmas.

November 1st, All Saints Day. No spells may be cast and all encounters with supernatural creatures are ignored today. If a character has received any wound or condition due to an encounter with a supernatural creature on the previous day, roll d6. On a 1-3, that condition or wound is miraculously healed (does not apply to witches).

Advent: Advent begins with Advent Sunday, which can fall between November 27th and December 3rd (use the date in your planner). All these Sundays until Christmas are Social Events, and weddings are forbidden.

December 24-25th, Christmas. Social event. Three masses are celebrated, beginning at midnight. Churches are decorated with holly, ivy or candles. Treat any supernatural encounter on Christmas day as an encounter with the Krampus (Danger 69).

December 26th, 27th and 28th (Saint Stephen, Saint John the Evangelist, the Holy Innocents). Social Events.

People of Status 1+ do not work during the period between Christmas and Epiphany (January 6th), exchanging gifts on January 1st, New Year's Day.

Events Track

Events Track

(Start Here) There are multiple signs of something awful happening in Eldritchwood. **A bad smell rises from the bogs.** Strange noises, lights and voices come from the woods. They say that **the King of Thorns** is determined to drive men out of his forest. Merchants and woodcutters won't pass through the forest anymore. Some got lost and came back a week later, aged as if 20 years had gone by. Maybe this is the result of angering **the Whispering Queen?**

The body of a missing girl is found, drained of all blood. Rumors say that in an attempt to preserve her once legendary beauty, the **Countess Elisabeth** is bathing in the blood of virgins.

Blood-curdling howls are heard throughout the night. A drunkard is found, shredded to bits, in a dark alley. **Strange markings**, painted in red, have appeared on a few doors.

You decide to investigate. You start the game by playing one of the following moves:

· Visit a Friend to discuss the events, and maybe switch to that character;
· Visit the Inn;
· Take a stroll through the forest;
· Investigate in town. You are trying to undertsand who is behind the supernatural attacks. For every 2 Clues you find, you may roll d6 on the list of Major Foes and eliminate that suspect from the list, narrowing the choice to a smaller number with every successful investigation.

On the following days, you may try any of the actions described in the actions chapter. Every day, there is a 3 in 6 chance of an event happening. When an event happens, roll d3 and add it to the Event Track and play the corresponding event listed here.

1-2) Neighbors fight. A farmer's goat got loose and ate vegetables in the neighbors' garden. Neighbors demand payment for the eaten crop or receive the goat as compensation for the damage suffered. You may intervene by playing Scene 1.

3) You catch a cold. Test Vigor vs. 2. On a success, nothing happens. On a failure, you'll be sick in bed and unable to act for a number of days equal to d6-Vigor (minimum of 1 day). While bedridden , you may still read, if you have books, but you cannot cast a spell or attend any social event. While sick, you may play a scene in which one of your contacts visits you, and switch control to that character, but then that contact must Test Vigor vs. 2 to avoid contracting the disease.

4) Guards bring a large torture instrument called an **Iron Maiden** into the main square, loudly proclaiming that a person would be placed there for violating the laws; when closing the door of this human-sized coffin, spikes would pierce the guilty person's skin until they realize the error of their ways. From now on, any characters who are tortured will resist with Disadvantage.

5) A week ago, a merchant hit a woman who stepped on his expensive shoes. The woman retaliated by pouring cold water on him. In the following days, the merchant fell ill and died. **The woman is accused of witchcraft**. In 1d6 days she will be judged. If you want, bail her out by paying 15 Gold and play Scene 2.

6) Witch torture. In a woman's yard, the neighbors saw an owl, late at night, glowing with an unnatural light. The authorities caught the woman, accusing her of witchcraft. The woman says the owl was just a bird flying by. No one believes her. They tie her to a chair in the main square, put large shoes on her feet and pour boiling water inside. If she screams in pain, she is a witch. If she is not, God will give her the strength to resist the pain. A crowd stands by. You may move along or watch (play Scene 3).

7) Meat disappears. You hear Frey the butcher screaming, He runs around with his head in his hands, shouting "All my meat is gone! Even the lamb that I bought yesterday from Countess Lucretia's farm. I opened the shop and there's nothing left, not even bones! What am I to do now? The store's locks are not broken". If you are playing as Frey the Butcher (24), go to Scene 5. If you are playing as another character, you may ignore the event or investigate by going to Scene 5.

8) Rats! You hear a cry from the street. A greengrocer is fighting off rats. A small crowd gathers but seems unable to act. To intervene, play Scene 4.

9-10) Inquisition. If you are Suspected of witchcraft,

94

Test Alertness vs. 1. Success: you are on your toes and nothing happens. On a failure: Guards try to catch you! Play scene 6.

11) Gossips. Someone is spreading lies about you in town. A friend of a friend told you so. If you don't stop the gossips, you will have Disadvantage on your next Charisma roll. Perform a Mind and a Charisma roll vs. 1. If one or both rolls fails, you can't find the culprit. If both rolls succeed, you find who is talking about you. Choose one of your enemies if you have any, or roll a random Notable if you don't have enemies listed in your character profile. If this person is a priest or someone of higher Status than you, there is nothing you can do. In all other cases, you may enter Social Combat with this person.

12) The gambler. A man tries to persuade you to play a game of dice. If you have at least 6 Gold, test your Will vs. his Charisma of 1 to avoid playing. If you do play, you can bet any number of Gold, then roll d6. You may use one reroll, if you have it, but only one. On a 1-3, you win. On a 4-6, the gambler wins and bids you farewell. If you have 5 or fewer Gold, ignore the gambler's request.

13-14) The thief. Someone bumps into you. Test Alertness vs. his Dexterity of 2. If you fail, you will later realize that he stole a leather pouch containing 1d6 Gold (or less if you had less than this). If you succeed, you may run away or play a combat encounter vs. a Violent Robber (Danger 61 on the Dangers list - decide if you want to fight before reading his profile).

15) A perfume shop opens. It sells perfumed oils and soaps, but obviously the prices are only for the well-off. It becomes fashionable to wear perfume to cover one's stench. All status 2+ people must spend at least 2 Gold or be at Disadvantage on their next Charisma roll.

16) Death of a Jester. You find a small ad on a stand that says "Fun Times, Central Square", and today's date. You look around but there's no jesters, acrobats or musicians. A small crowd has gathered in the square and is discussing vigorously. You hear that Barn the jester died suddenly before the performance, so they canceled the performance. Local vendors are discussing yesterday's scandal in the Tavern. Allegedly Barn quarreled with Louise, the tavern worker, and this morning he was found dead.

He choked on bread. If you want to investigate this matter, play Scene 8.

17) Rat infestation. Passers-by rush to the market square, looking very excited. From a man, you learn that the rats attacked, ate fruits and gnawed the apple seller to the bone. "Today, poison will be scattered everywhere, so if you have animals, keep them indoors. Damn rats...", the man hastily leaves. If you want to investigate, play Scene 9.

18) Dance plague. One lady suddenly begins to dance, even if there is no music. She seems unable to stop, as if her body is possessed by a malevolent spirit. You may ignore this event (you tell yourself she's gone crazy) or investigate (play Scene 10).

19) A werewolf has attacked a woman. A man completely covered with hair, has attacked a woman, biting her arm. Then he ran towards a farm. Local residents light torches and pursue the beast. You may ignore the event, grab a torch and join the villagers (go to Scene 11) or investigate on your own (go to Scene 13).

20) The tatzelwurm, a flying snake with a cat's head, has been sighted in the Eldritchwood forest. If you want, you may hunt it and play Danger 55.

21-22) The mysterious traveler. Play Danger 22 from the Dangers section.

23-24) A Chance Encounter. Roll d66 on the list of Notables. Reroll if you roll your character's number. You randomly meet that Notable and have a chance to interact with him/her, for example playing the Befriend, Court or Challenge to Duel action.

25-26) Danger! While running some errands, something bad happens to you. Choose: roll d66 on the Dangers list and play that encounter, or roll 2d6 instead of d3 for your next Event roll.

27) Unavoidable Danger! Roll d66 on the Dangers list and play that encounter.

28) A Moment of Respite. All is calm. You may roll d6 if you want and subtract the result from the Events Track number. If this brings you to an Event that has already been played, ignore it – nothing happens.

29) The Green Children. Villagers are discussing something in the main square. Coming closer you see that hunters have caught carry an unusually large wolf. Two hunters lead a boy and a girl. The children hiss among themselves in an incomprehensible language. Their skin is greenish and they are wearing expensive outfits.
A woman says: "These are the children of the fairies. They were given food, but they did not like it."
If you want to interact with the green children, play Scene 19.

30) The Swamp Drake has been sighted. You may play a Hunt scene with the character you are currently playing or switch to one of your Contacts. This creature is EXTREMELY dangerous - many strong men have tried to slay the beast and have never returned from the bogs.

31) Ravens. As you walk near town, cawing noises attract your attention. Play an encounter with Ravens (Danger 45) or advance the Event track number by 1d6.

32) Black Market offer. A shady fellow offers you to buy (choose one of the following): a Silver Dagger for 12 Gold, a Pair of Fancy Gloves for 4 Gold, a Delicacy for 3 Gold, a Bottle of Fine Wine for 6 Gold, a Grimoire for 20 Gold, a Heavy Mace for 6 Gold. The price seems too good to be true. Probably it's stolen stuff. If you choose to buy, add +1 to the next Track Event number you roll.

33) Black Market offer. A shady fellow offers you to buy (choose one of the following): a Silver Dagger for 11 Gold, a Pair of Fancy Gloves for 3 Gold, a Delicacy for 2 Gold, a Bottle of Fine Wine for 5 Gold, a Grimoire for 15 Gold, an Iron Amulet Against the Fae for 8 Gold, a Heavy Mace for 5 Gold. The price seems too good to be true. Probably it's stolen stuff. If you choose to buy, add +2 to the next Track Event number you roll.

34) A Beast has been sighted. Choose one of the following Dangers: the Basilisk (Danger 12), the Tatzelwurm (Danger 55), the Tree of Terror (Danger 56), the Nachtzehrer (Danger 41), the Swamp Drake (Danger 52). You may attempt to Hunt this creature. If you slay the creature, in addition to any reward stated in its description, you can apply a -1 to the next Event roll (with a minimum result of 1).

35) A Lunatic attacks You. Play Danger 32.

36) Price of firewood increases. As a result, people start to use less wood to warm water, and take less care of their personal hygiene. You may either pay 1 Gold now, or have Disadvantage on the first Vigor roll to resist a disease you will roll from now on.

37) Stolen Chicken. The old witch, One-eyed Mary, has stolen a few chickens from a farmer. If you want to investigate, spend 2 Clues to locate One-Eyed Mary and then play an encounter with her (Danger 42 on the Dangers list). If you defeat her, you recover the chickens and the farmer will give you a Delicacy or a Bottle of Fine Wine (choose). Ignore this event if One-Eyed Mary has already been killed in this game.

38) A Woman Plunges to Death. As you walk through the village, a woman falls from a window on the third story. If you want, you can try to save her by rolling Dexterity vs. 2. If you succeed, play Scene 16. If you fail or do not intervene, the woman dies in front of you, and you add +1 to the next Event Track roll.

39) Unavoidable Danger! Roll d66 on the list of Dangers and play that encounter.

40) Hunting Restrictions. Due to a new law passed, no character may Hunt in the next 3d6 days. The restriction does not apply to the hunting of supernatural beasts. If you decide to hunt illegally during this period, perform an Alertness vs. 2 roll. If you succeed, nothing happens. If you fail, you are caught and must pay a 10 Gold fine. If you do not pay, play an encounter with Guards (Danger 23 on the Dangers list).

41) You meet a Woman of Ill Repute. Play Danger 76.

42) You encounter a mysterious stranger on the road. Play Danger 68.

43) There's something about silk. All wealthy ladies start to buy silk, as lice and fleas do not cling to silk.

If you are a Status 2+ character, you must spend at least 5 Gold to buy silk goods. If you spend at least 10 Gold, your house and person are protected from lice - you can ignore any event which implies lice infestation.

44) A blacksmith is recruiting a few people to teach them his profession. If you want to qualify, you must have a minimum of Vigor 2. Test Charisma vs. 0. If you succeed, you are hired. You must sign a contract where you promise that for 10 years you can't drink alcohol, be late for training, gamble, or stare at the master's wife, sister or daughter. If you are Status 0 and you are hired, after 6 months you will be considered Status 1. No advantage for characters who are already Status 1 or better. If you break the contract by performing any of the forbidden actions, you lose the Status.

45) A Witch is sighted. Apparently someone saw a woman tracing mysterious signs on the ground near an old oak by the road that leads to the forest. You may ignore this event (add 1 to the next Event roll) or go to investigate (play Scene 17).

46) Rats in your House. You may ignore this Event if you are playing as Crisanta, if you have a Loyal Dog, a Splendid Housecat or a Weasel. In all other cases, fight an encounter with Rats (Danger 77) and lose 1d6 Gold, in house repairs and stolen food. If you can't afford repairs, you will get Disadvantage to your next 3 Charisma rolls.

47) Mermaid sighted. A mermaid was seen bathing in a small pond in the forest. If you want to Investigate, play Scene 18.

48) The Swamp Drake has been sighted. You may play a Hunt scene with your current character or switch to one of your Contacts. This beast (Danger 52) is EXTREMELY dangerous - many men have tried to slay it and have never returned from the bogs.

49) Mandrake in the forest. You may go searching for this fabulous plant. If you do, play Danger 79.

50) A storyteller from another village causes a bit of stir by telling salacious stories. People are laughing, but the authorities are irked. You may speak with the man by playing Scene 20.

51) A street corner salesman has gotten ill and asks you to take over his business for a week, while he recovers. He will give you 50% of the profit done in that week. You may ignore this if it seems risky or inappropriate. If you accept, play Scene 21.

52) A traveling doctor visits the village for 2 days. If you are suffering from any Condition, you may ask him to visit you, paying a fee in Gold equal to 3 times your Status (minimum 3 Gold). If you do so, play Scene 12.

53) A cobbler is being flogged on the main square. Apparently, he badly repaired shoes which caused a girl to fall and break a toe. If you want to intervene, read Scene 22.

54) A Fire. A wooden house caught fire, and the fire is spreading to nearby houses. Decide if you want to help (it may be dangerous) then play Scene 23.

55) A farmer is whipping his wife for disobedience. He explains that it is better for the Salvation of her Soul. The woman doesn't seem to agree. If you want to intervene, play Scene 24.

56) Grimoire for sale. You hear of someone offering a Grimoire for sale, for 20 Gold. This Grimoire contains a single random spell. You may buy it if you want, at no risk to you. Determine the spell after purchase.

57) Grimoire for sale. You hear of someone offering a Grimoire for sale, for 40 Gold. This Grimoire contains three random spells. You may buy it if you want. Determine which spells it contains after purchase.

58) A Beast was sighted. Choose one of the following Dangers: Jack Frost (Danger 25, you may select this only in winter), the Basilisk (Danger 12), the Tatzelwurm (Danger 55), the Tree of Terror (Danger 56), the Nachtzehrer (Danger 41), the Swamp Drake (Danger 52), the Guardian of Wheat (Danger 73), a Barrow Cat (Danger 78). You may Hunt this creature. DO NOT READ THE DESCRIPTION OF THE CREATURE UNTIL YOU HAVE DECIDED. Exception: If you have a Bestiary, read up to THREE descriptions of your choice before deciding which beast you want to Hunt, if any.

59) Rat invasion. As the town is overrun by hordes of hungry rats, several Notables are attacked. You and all of your Contacts must play Danger 77. Each character should play the encounter separately. Roll d6 for you, then for your contacts in any order desired, If any character rolls a 1, that character must also fight Blackheart (Danger 67). All characters with a Splendid Cat, a Loyal Dog or a Ferret can reroll 1 die in this combat, but if the reroll is a 1, the pet is killed by rats. You may acquire a new pet during the next General Market day.

Later on the same day, **Peddlers** announce that they would go from house to house and exchange things. If you have an item you don't need, you can barter it for something else of your choice, as long as its Gold value is the same or lower (as shown under the General Market action), or you can spend extra Gold to pay for the difference in cost.

60) A Chance meeting. You may interact with a random Notable. Roll d66 to determine who. You may play the Befriend Someone action if you want.

61) Witch Ladder attack. Test your Alertness vs. 3. If you succeed, you find a witch's ladder under your bed, you throw it out and you are fine. If you fail, you will die after a number of days equal to the sum of your Will+Vigor. You may investigate to discover who cursed you. You'll need to spend 3 Clues and then play Scene 25. If you die, you may continue the investigation with any Notable that was your contact, passing any Clues you may have gathered to the new investigator.

62) Spiritual Assault. A shadow creature attacks you in your sleep! Fight against a foe with 2 in all Attributes. You may not escape from this fight. If you have a Talisman against Shadows, you can ignore this event. If you are attacked and survive, you may investigate to discover who sent the shadow figure to kill you. You'll need to spend 3 Clues and then play Scene 25. If you die, you may decide that one of your contacts finds your body and may investigate, using the same rules (3 Clues to play Scene 25).

63)Assassination attempt. Play Danger 16. If you defeat the Assassin, gain 1 Clue. The assassin does not know who sent her to kill you, but you might understand by putting Clues together (spend 3 Clues to reveal the identity of a random Notable, then come up with a logical explanation for that person wanting you dead).

64) A Secret Word. A woman proposes to reveal to you a Secret Word if you give her 1 Special Item or 15 Gold. You may ignore her or buy the Secret Word.

65) A Mandrake Root. A peasant offers you a mandrake root for 15 Gold. You may buy it or ignore the offer. If you buy, increase the next Event roll by 1.

66) Loss of coin. You lose 1 Gold. You look everywhere, but the coin is lost. If you have no coins when this Event happens, play Scene 14.

67) Loss of coins. You lose d6 Gold. You look everywhere, but the coins are lost. If you have no coins when this Event happens, play Scene 14.

68) Loss of an important Item. Choose one Special Item on your play sheet and delete it. Feel free to invent a story reason for your loss.

69) Loss of a random Item. Roll a d6 for every Special Item you own, re-rolling ties. You lose the item with the lowest score. Feel free to invent a story reason for your loss. Maybe something broke, was stolen or gnawed by rats.

70) Flooding. Your house is flooded. You might lose books. Roll a 1 in 6 chance that every Grimoire or Bestiary you possess is lost. You may spend 1 Fate to prevent this loss (1 Fate per book you save).

71) Earwax trouble. The government has issued one edict forbidding people to wash their ears for some time, to collect earwax. Earwax is used to create painter's colors. You may comply or not. If you comply, for the next 2d6 days you will roll all Alertness tests for hearing at a Disadvantage. If you do not comply and are caught by guards for any reason, you will have to pay a fine of 2d6 Gold, or spend 1d6 days in prison if you can't pay.

72) Spice price spike. Double the cost of buying Delicacies for the remainder of the game.

73) Honey Trouble. Bees are dying. Double the cost of a Jar of Honey for the rest of the game.

74) A Chance Meeting for Lunch. Roll d66 to select a random Notable. You may attempt to Befriend that person, but you must use 6 Gold, a Bottle of Fine

Events Track

Wine, a Jar of Honey or a Delicacy in the process.

75) Joust. A group of knights arrives to hold a jousting tournament, drawing spectators from across the land. If you own a suit of armor or a helmet and shield, or if you have enough coin to buy them now, you may participate. Perform 3 combat encounters against knights (use the Guards attributes, Danger 23, but ignore the special rules about capture). If you win all the encounters you win the tournament. If you win, you gain 3 universal rerolls and Advantage to your next 3 Charisma rolls. All wounds inflicted during the tournament are not fatal and will heal in 1 day per point of Attribute lost.

76) New Chapel. A group of villagers come together to build a new chapel, bringing the community together for a common goal. If you want to contribute, you can give 4 x Status in Gold, gaining Advantage to your next 2 Charisma tests. After 2d6 days, the work for the chapel will start. If you want to supervise, play Scene 26.

77) A Secret Word. A random Notable proposes to reveal to you a Secret Word for 20 Gold and your most expensive Special Item. You may ignore this request or buy the Secret Word. If you buy, you may add that Notable as a Contact.

78) Pilgrimage. A group of pilgrims passes through the village on their way to a holy site. You may join them. If you join them, the character leaves play for 30 days. Test Vigor vs. 1 three times. If any Vigor test fails, you die during the trip. If you survive, you return with 1 Holy Relic and 1 Vial of Holy Water. Whatever the success of the pilgrimage, if you accept it, you gain 1 Fate point at the end of the 30 days.

79) Drought. A terrible drought strikes the village, causing crops to wither and livestock to die. Double the cost of any food (including Honey and Delicacies), drink or livestock until the end of the game. The price of pets (housecats, dogs, ferrets) will not increase.

80) Disease. Test Vigor vs. 2 or catch disentery. This will give you -1 to Vigor and all Social rolls for 1d6 days. You may reduce this by 1 day by visiting the apothecary or herbalist and spending 1 Gold.

81) The relic. You have a chance to find a Holy relic. You must go to the forest, following a voice in your head, and play 3 random Dangers. If you survive, at the end of the ordeal you will find a Holy Relic in a clearing. You may ignore this event, or pass it onto one of your Contacts and play it with that character.

82) An edict is passed: nobody can visit the forest on odd days. All forest activities (taking a stroll, hunting, picking mushrooms, gathering firewood, looking for rare herbs) are now forbidden on odd days. A roll of 1 on d6 on odd days means playing Danger 23.

83) A demon attacks you! Play Danger 34. If you win, you find a Holy Relic not far from the place where you were attacked.

84) An aura of gloom descends upon you. During your next combat encounter, you may not escape.

85) Plague Rats. You and all of your Contacts must play Danger 77. Increase the rats' Vigor to 2. Roll d6 for you, then for your contacts in any order desired, If any character rolls a 1 or 2, that character must also fight Blackheart the King of Rats (Danger 67). Characters with a Splendid Cat, a Loyal Dog or a Ferret can reroll 1 die in this combat, but if the reroll is a 1, the pet is killed by rats. You may acquire a new pet during the next General Market day. Any character wounded by rats must Test Vigor vs. 1 or contract a disease that will make it impossible to heal any wounds (loss of Vigor or Dexterity) for the next 3d6 days.

86) Holy Vision. If you do not know any spells and are wounded, all your wounds or conditions are miraculously healed and you gain 1 Clue. If you know one or more spells, test Will vs. 3. If you fail, you lose 1 spell of your choice (if you still have the Grimoire, you may learn the spell again in the usual manner).

87) Church under attack. You have the chance to help a small church in the forest, sieged by undead creatures. Decide if you want to help or ignore the event, then play Scene 27.

88) Switched Item. Choose a random special item from your play sheet, and exchange it with any special item possessed by another character you controlled during this game. If you didn't control any other character or if all other characters have no items, just delete a random item from your play sheet.

89) Evil Comes Knocking at your Door. Play one round of combat (rolling 3 dice as usual) against the Main Foe of this game (if you didn't discover his/her identity yet, roll d6 to select a Major Foe). Fight only once. After this "round" of combat, the creature disappears. If you defeat the foe, you win the game!

90) You are caught by the Inquisition. If you have any Grimoire or Amulet, you will be tortured. Test Will vs. 3. If you succeed, you are released, but your books are destroyed. If you fail, you are put to death. If you have any Clues, you can scream them while you die, thus passing them onto the next played character.

91) Curse of Bad Health. From now on, all healing will fail. Characters may recover lost points of Vigor or Dexterity only by using the Healing spell or by sacrificing 1 Holy Relic.

92) Mysterious Death. Select a random Notable. That Notable is found dead. If this is your current character, you die but manage to leave a document with all your unspent Clues, that one of your contacts may pick up.

93) Army of Rats. Play Danger 77 three times in a row. If you are wounded, test Vigor vs. 2 or contract the black death. If you are infected, you will automatically die after 2d6+Vigor days. There is no cure. Any character you get in contact with must test Vigor or suffer the same fate.

94) Epidemic of Black Death. Your current character, any character you interact with, and any character you switch to, must test Vigor vs. 2 or contract the black death. All infected characters die after 2d6+Vigor days. There is no cure.

95) Panic Attack. Test Will vs. 3. If you fail, you may no longer use Fate points on this character until the end of the game.

96) Night Terrors. Perform 3 tests of Will vs. 3. Lose 1 Vigor per every failure. If this brings your character's Vigor to 0, you die of heart failure in the night, and the game ends with a victory for the forces of evil.

97) Direct Attack. Select 1 random Notable. That person disappears, never to be found again. If you select your current character, the game ends and you lose.

98) Desperate Times. Select 3 random Notables. Their bodies are found, lifeless and with an expression of pure terror on their faces. These may include the character you are currently playing - if that happens, you lose the game.

99) The End Times are Nigh. You realize that you have 3 days to destroy the Main Foe. If you don't, the forces of evil will triumph.

100) This is the End. If you reach this event, the game ends with a victory for the forces of evil. You may play the game again, starting from scratch, but this time the forces of evil have triumphed.

Events Track

Scenes

Scenes are small events that you read, and play, only when an Event sends you to the corresponding number.

Scene 1) You may calm down the fighting villagers with a successful Charisma roll vs. their Will of 1. If you succeed, you may alter the next Event roll by 1 either upwards or downwards. If you fail, you are caught in a fight and must perform a Dexterity roll vs. their Vigor of 1. On a failure, you lose 1 Vigor (this is just a punch or kick and cannot kill you: if your Vigor goes to 0, you are knocked out cold for 1 day, and wake up fully healed on the next day). On a success, you dodge the punch and leave the villagers to their quarrelsome ways.

Scene 2) The following day, **you find a Grimoire** on your doorstep. This is a leather-bound tome full of magic formulas, diagrams and recipes. You may keep it or destroy it. In any case, add +1 to the next Event roll. If you keep it, when you read it refer to the Spells section to determine which spells it contains.

Scene 3) You can save the woman from torture by passing a Charisma test vs.3. If you roll a 1, however, you will become Suspected of siding with witches. If your roll succeeds, the woman will be freed and on the following morning someone will leave a reward by your door. Roll d6:

1. 1) A Delicacy and a Pot of Honey.
2. A Bestiary.
3. 2d6 Gold coins or a Sturdy Shield (choose).
4. A Fancy Hat appropriate to your Status and gender.
5. A Silver Dagger or a Good Helmet (choose).
6. A random Grimoire or a piece of parchment with a Secret Word written on it (choose).

Scene 4) Fight the rats (Danger 77). If you are playing with Crisanta, you automatically win this encounter. If you win, the greengrocer rewards you with 1 Delicacy.

Scene 5) You try to understand what happened to the meat. Every day, test Alertness vs. 1. For every success, gain 1 Meat Clue. Once you have 3 Meat Clues, play

Scene 28. You may at any moment abort this investigation.

Scene 6) Run from Inquisitors. Play Guards (Danger 23 on the Dangers list) – you need to escape successfully. Running away from them automatically makes you guilty. If they catch you, you will be tortured for 1d6 days and then put to death 2d6 days later – but you can play a rescue action with any of your contacts to free you and they can even pool their resources (you could have one character cast a spell and another rescue you, or they could pool their Gold to bribe someone). If they put your character to death, add +3 to the next Events roll.

Scene 7) This Scene does not exist! If you are reading this, you must have committed some sin. You immediately become Suspect of Witchcraft.

Scene 8) You may discover Louise's Secret spending 2 Clues. When you do, you get to decide whether she killed the man or was unjustly accused, and whether you are going to accuse her or not. If you ARE Louise, you may spend 2 Clues to investigate on the real cause of the man's death and clear yourself. If you do not clear yourself, you become Suspected.

Scene 9) If you have any pets (Loyal Dog, Splendid Housecat, Ferret) you must roll a 1 in 6 chance of losing them due to the poisoned food that's been spread to kill rats. If you lose a pet, you will be Morose for d6 days. You may replace your pet, buying a new one, only after you stop being Morose.

Scene 10) You find the woman and she's indeed shaking and gyrating. She doesn't have a happy expression, as you would expect from someone dancing for fun. This seems like something different. Resist contracting the dancing disease by rolling Vigor vs.2. On a failure, you are infected and also your contacts must roll, then the contacts of your contacts, until eventually all the Notables are infected.

Anyone infected will waste 1d6+2 days dancing, and will be at -1 on Dexterity or Vigor, your choice, at the end of the process. The loss will take 12- Vigor days of rest to heal.

Scene 11) You join the villagers. If you want, you can meet a random Notable in the crowd, or you can call one of your Contacts in the scene and switch to that

101

character. You find nothing at the farm - just a drunk man sleeping on a heap of hay. You wake him up, but he seems too drunk to have noticed any movement around the farm. You may return to the village or wait for the rest of the villagers to return home and try to question the man as he recovers from his drunken stupor (go to Scene 15).

Scene 12) You pay but there is no effect on your condition. You are convinced the man is a fraud.

Scene 13) You investigate on your own. You might spend 1 Clue to find the werewolf, or test Alertness vs.2. On a success, play Danger 65.

Scene 14) Someone understands you are penniless and suggests you to visit the moneylender (Danger 36). You may use this option ONLY if you do not owe money to the moneylender already. In this case, the moneylender is willing to negotiate his usual terms and conditions. You may use one of the following benefits: 1) The surcharge applied by the money lender is only 5%, repaid after 10 days; 2) The moneylender will let you borrow up to 60 Gold; 3) The moneylender will give you his standard terms, but you will have 20 days (not 10) to repay your debt.

Scene 15) As you question the man, test your Alertness vs.1. You have to play Danger 65. If your Alertness test was successful, treat this as a normal fight. If your Alertness test failed, you may not use any rerolls in this combat encounter.

Scene 16) With amazing agility, you manage to catch the woman in your arms before she hits the ground! The woman thanks you and gives you (choose one of the following): a Bottle of Fine Wine, 3 Gold, or a Delicacy. It seems she was startled when she heard a cat on the roof speaking with a human voice. If you want to catch the cat, you must perform a Dexterity roll vs. 2. If you fail, you fall down and take 2 Wounds. If you succeed, you manage to see a strange cat giving you an almost human glance and then disappearing into thin air. Gain 1 Clue.

Scene 17) You quickly find the woman and indeed she looks like she is practicing magic. As you spy on her, you realize she has noticed your presence. Play Danger 70, the Wandering Witch.

Scene 18) Perform an Alertness roll vs. 2. On a success, you find the pond of the mermaid (play Danger 80). On a failure, you can try again after 1d6 days, but if you fail again, you will give up. On a roll of 1, you run into some unexpected danger. Roll d66 and play the Danger corresponding to the number rolled.

Scene 19) You try to talk to the children, but they don't speak your language. You may spend money (5 Gold per week) to keep them fed and have someone try to teach them to speak. Every week, you may test Charisma vs.1. On a success, you befriend the children. After d6 weeks, the children will speak well enough to reveal their Secret - read Scene 29.

Scene 20) The storyteller tells you a lot of interesting bits about life in the village. Gain 1 Clue about a random Notable. If that Notable has no Secret, you may use this Clue to Blackmail the Notable. For your silence, you gain a number of Gold equal to the character's Status, with a minimum of 1.

Scene 21) Test Mind vs. 2. On a success, you gain 1d6 Gold in a week of work. On a failure, nothing happens. On a natural roll of 1, some merchandise is shoplifted while you are on duty, and you must repay 2 Gold to the merchant at the end of the week.

Scene 22). If you are Status 2 or higher, or if you pass a Mind and a Charisma test vs. 2 you can save the cobbler from the punishment. If you succeed, the cobbler will thank you with a Fine Pair of Shoes. If you fail, no-one listens to your plea. If you roll a 1, guards will try to fine you 2 Gold for disorderly conduct. If you refuse to pay, they will try to catch you (see Danger 23). If you or some of your friends do not pay the fine and the Guards catch you, you will also be flogged and be at -1 on Dexterity or Vigor (your choice) for d6 days, until your wounds heal.

Scene 23) Test Vigor vs. 2. On a failure, you aren't helpful. On a success, your contribution to fighting the fire is relevant and the family thanks you with a Delicacy. On a roll of 1, your clothes catch fire and you will have to rest for 2d6 days to heal from the burns. During this rest period the only activity you can perform is Reading.

Scene 24). If you are Status 2 or higher, or if you pass a Charisma roll vs. 1 you can calm the farmer and save the woman from the punishment. If you succeed, the woman will thank you profusely and, after the ruckus has ended, she will give you an Amulet saying she fashioned it herself for you. You may accept it or refuse it. If you fail, the farmer does not listen to your plea. If you roll a 1, the farmer will try to hit you with a spade – play one Combat vs. a farmer with Vigor 1 and Dexterity 1. This will be a non-lethal combat (you may not die as result of this encounter) and all wounds caused will heal in d6 days.

Scene 25) Invent a reason why a witch should hate you or want you dead… maybe she was paid by one of your enemies? You may play the Accusation action, accusing the witch OR your enemy, or play an encounter with Danger 70 (ignore the part where the witch may help you, she will fight). If you defeat the witch, you can find the loot described under Danger 70 or 1 Secret Word or 2 Clues (your choice).

Scene 26) As you supervise the foundations of the chapel, a group of brigands tries to steal the building materials and valuable tools. If you intervene, you must fight against a single bandit (play Danger 11). If you do not win this combat, the bandits steal materials and the construction of the new chapel is delayed. During the next 60 days, you may not attend Church on Sundays as you will be busy with this project. You may participate in other Social Events. Once the construction of the chapel is completed, you may take 1 vial of Holy Water every Sunday without leaving an offer.

Scene 27) Roll d6. On a 1-3, play Danger 54, but you gain Advantage to your Will tests. On a 4-6, play Danger 53. If you win, gain 3 vials of Holy Water or the ability to borrow a Holy Relic for 2d6 days (you must return the relic to the church at the end of that period).

Scene 28) Someone is apparently using the meat to feed a werewolf hiding in a dark alley. You may call one of your Contacts and send him/her to deal with the werewolf or face the creature yourself (play Danger 65), or ignore the whole story but add +2 to the next Event roll.

Scene 29. You discover the Secret of the Green Children. If you already discovered who is the Major Foe who is attacking Eldritchwood, from the words of the children (who escaped from that Major Foe) you gain 3 rerolls that you can use during the final confrontation. You may also pass these rerolls onto

another character if you wish, by playing the Visiting a Friend action (you visit a friend and reveal the secret). If you did not find out who is the Major Foe yet, roll d6 on the list of Major Foes and exclude the corresponding foe.

Eldritchwood - Character Sheet

Name		Gold	Status

Vigor	Dexterity	Mind	Charisma	Will	Alertness

Milestones

Traits

Contacts